Enjoy the book & then the film

JUROR NUMBER 2

love
A.
xx

JUROR NUMBER 2

THE STORY OF A MURDER,
THE AGONY OF A NEIGHBORHOOD

Efrem Sigel

THE WRITERS' PRESS
New York, NY

Copyright © 2020 by Efrem Sigel.

All rights reserved. No part of this book may be used, reproduced or stored in any form whatsoever without written permission of the publisher, except in the case of brief quotations embodied in critical reviews.

The Writers' Press, New York, NY
Juror Number 2: The Story of a Murder, the Agony of a Neighborhood
by Efrem Sigel

Publisher's Cataloging-In-Publication Data
(Prepared by The Donohue Group, Inc.)

    Name: Sigel, Efrem, author.
       Title: Juror number 2: the story of a murder, the agony of a neighborhood / Efrem Sigel.
       Other Titles: Juror number two
       Description: New York: The Writers' Press, 2020
       Identifiers: ISBN 978-1-73242-552-1 (hardcover)
               ISBN 978-1-73242-550-7 (paperback)
               ISBN 978-1-73242-551-4 (ebook)
      Summary: "This riveting memoir recounts the author's experience on a jury in a murder trial and his subsequent investigation of the conditions in East Harlem that led young people to be involved in drug-selling and criminal activity. Besides the trial itself, the book is the story of the failures in NYCHA housing projects, the schools and the criminal justice system, and the efforts of a handful of educators, nonprofit leaders and criminal justice reformers to find pathways to success for these young people"—Provided by publisher.
      1. Trials (Murder)—New York (State)—New York. 2. Jurors—New York (State)—New York—Biography. 3. Youth and violence—New York (State)—New York. 4. East Harlem (New York, N.Y.)—Social conditions. 5. Sigel Efrem.

Classification: LCC HV9106.N6 S54 2020 (print)
              LCC HV9106.N6 (ebook)
              DDC 364.36097471—dc23

Library of Congress Control Number: 2020935076

10 9 8 7 6 5 4 3 2 1

Published by The Writers' Press, New York, NY.
Contact: queries.thewriterspress@gmail.com

For
Dimitres Pantelidis, Bennett Lieberman,
Mark Goldsmith, Omar Jackson
and so many others, in honor of their dedication to
improving opportunities for young people in East Harlem

PREFACE

This is a story about a brutal and senseless murder in East Harlem, New York, about the ensuing trial—in which I served as a juror—and about my subsequent search for why. Why the young men caught up in the trial were cutting school, joining gangs, selling drugs, getting arrested and spending years in jail. And how and why the failures of the New York City schools, its public housing projects and its criminal justice system, contributed to these outcomes.

Though jury service is required by law, it is relatively easy to dodge. Until The People vs. Abraham Cucuta, the trial that is the subject of this book, I had been called for jury duty half a dozen times. Only once before was I actually put in the jury box to be questioned by a judge and by opposing counsel. In that instance, after claiming that I couldn't be objective, I was quickly excused.

This time was different.

Jury duty is the one civic obligation that gives you, the juror, the opportunity to personally decide a matter of public concern: the guilt or innocence of an accused person. True, voting in an election has a direct bearing on public policy but voting is anonymous and voluntary, and it's the very rare instance where your lone vote decides an election.

As a juror in a criminal trial, however, your vote is one of 12 determining whether the accused goes free or is punished. For days, or in our case weeks, you listen to lawyers ask their questions, you watch and assess the witnesses as they give their answers—and as often as you like, you look straight at the defendant. When the charge is murder, you never forget that a decision to convict can take away his liberty for the rest of his life.

Quite naturally, I had thought that our jury's vote at the conclusion of the trial would be the end of the story. But I was mistaken. For me the jury verdict was only the beginning.

ACKNOWLEDGMENTS

This book would not have been possible without the cooperation of many people. I especially want to single out: Vanessa Cruz, who spoke bravely to a convicted murderer and who patiently answered my many questions about her family and the neighborhood; Dimitres Pantelidis, the peerless principal of PS/IS 171 Patrick Henry; Bennett Lieberman, the principal of Central Park East High School, who turned a failing school into a success; Mark Goldsmith, the visionary founder of Getting Out and Staying Out, with his highly effective ways of connecting with "the guys" at Rikers and post-Rikers; and Omar Jackson, the director of SAVE, who strives to keep the peace in East Harlem. My heartfelt thanks go to them and to the many others who helped and who are listed here.

Fellow jurors and alternates: Especially Marc Dolfman, Harvey Lipkis, Emily Lundell and Kristen Roeckle; also Sam Captan, Joselina Goris, Sophia Heydebrand, Christen Johansen, Olivia Pinney, Miguel Semidey; alternates Melissa Cohen and John Koch

Judge, attorneys, DA office staff, family contacts

New York State Supreme Court: Judge Michael Obus and court attorney Daniel Rosen

Defense attorney: Dawn M. Florio; Fred Lichtmacher, plaintiff's attorney and Florio colleague

Manhattan District Attorney's Office: Roxanne Leong, Emily Tuttle and Caitlyn Fowles, media relations

Family members: Maria Torres, mother of the late Manuel Sabater; Vanessa Cruz, niece of the late Manuel Sabater; Varda Yoran, mother of Assistant District Attorney Dafna Yoran

NYPD PSA 5: Amir Yakatally, deputy inspector, commander; Detective Angel Lujan and Sergeant Michael Vega, Community Affairs. Precinct 23: Detectives Joshua Berish and Billy Dunn

Elected official: State Assemblyman Robert Rodriguez

Educators

PS 171 Patrick Henry: Dimitres Pantelidis, principal; Neris Roldan and Rachel Cohn, teachers

Central Park East High School: Bennett Lieberman, principal; Valerie Wald, teacher

Success Academy Harlem 3: Tara Stant, principal; Brian Whitley, (former) media relations

Dream and Dream Charter School: Rich Berlin, executive director; Eve Colavito; chief education officer; Emily Parkey, (former) managing director, family engagement; Alexandra Brown, teacher

PS 37 River East: Michael Panetta, principal

PS 83 Luis Munoz Rivera: Susan Kowal, teacher
PS 375 Mosaic Prep: Lisette Caesar, principal
Esperanza Preparatory Academy (middle and high school): Audrey Fowler, teacher
Manhattan Village Academy: Hector Geager, principal
East Side Community High School: Mark Federman, principal
Cristo Rey Brooklyn: William Henson, president; Joseph Dugan, principal
MESA Charter High School: Arthur Samuels, executive director; Pagee Cheung, principal
Parents, Community Education Council members (city-wide): Lisa Torres, Denikqua Berry, Claudia Perez, Ilene Brettler, Maud Maron, Naomi Peña, Thomas Wrocklage, Leonard Silverman
NYCHA: Valeria Munt, deputy press secretary
NYC Independent Budget Office: Doug Turetsky, chief of staff, Sarita Subramanian; supervising analyst
Mayor's Office of Criminal Justice: Alacia Lauer (former) communications director
Nonprofit and community organizations
Getting Out and Staying Out (GOSO): Mark Goldsmith, (retired) CEO, founder; Geoff Golia, chief administrative and program officer; Julia Friedman, senior program director; Kristin Pulkkinen, chief development officer
SAVE (Stand Against Violence-East Harlem: Omar Jackson, director; Javon Alexander, supervisor
SCAN (Supportive Children's Advocacy Network): Lew Zuchman, executive director
Exodus Transitional Community: Julio Medina, founder, CEO; Kathleen Bernier, vice president, policy and communications; Nora Reissig, vice president, development and programs; Michael Luciano and David Hobert, board members
Union Settlement: David Nocenti, executive director; Susan Puder, director, development and communications; Delores Mims, director, early childhood education
LSA Family Health Service: Asari Beale, director of communications
Concrete Safaris: Mac Levine, executive director
East Harlem Tutorial Project: Efrain Guerrero, chief of staff; Alison Blazey, manager, data and research
Henry Street Settlement: David Garza, president, CEO
Pinkerton Foundation: Laurie Dien, vice president/executive director for programs; April Glad, senior program officer
Editorial, marketing, design
Lon Kirschner, cover design; Susan Ahlquist, book design; Kimberly Peticolas, copyediting, marketing
Readers: Max Byrd, Wendy Kopp, Laurie Dien, Joseph Johnson, Mark Singer, John Lescroart, Patty Machir
Most honest and sympathetic critic: Frederica Sigel

CONTENTS

Introduction	13
CHAPTER 1 The Dice Game	15
CHAPTER 2 The Most Serious Case You Could Imagine	18
CHAPTER 3 The Trial	25
CHAPTER 4 Gabriel Washington	31
CHAPTER 5 Alejandro Alvarez	40
CHAPTER 6 Summing Up: The Lawyers	54
CHAPTER 7 Our Turn	60
CHAPTER 8 Speaking to a Convicted Murderer	69
CHAPTER 9 The Search for Why: NYCHA and East River Houses	73
CHAPTER 10 The NYPD	81
CHAPTER 11 The East Harlem Schools	86
Charter Schools in District 4	95
Pathways to Educational Success	99
Leadership at the Top: A Tale of Three Chancellors	105
CHAPTER 12 The Nonprofit Role in East Harlem	111
CHAPTER 13 Criminal Justice Reform	119
CHAPTER 14 Afterword: Jurors, Lawyer, the Judge	128
CHAPTER 15 A Letter and Some Answers	133
Index	140
About the Author	143

INTRODUCTION

On a sunny, chilly day in early April, Omar Jackson and Javon Alexander, two black men in their 40s, talk matter of factly to me about their backgrounds—drug selling, violence and incarceration—not to boast, but to explain how they've come by the credentials needed for their job. That job is to curtail and interrupt violence in Johnson and Jefferson Houses, two large public housing projects in East Harlem.

Jackson is the program manager and Alexander the outreach worker supervisor of SAVE (Stand Against Violence East Harlem), a program run by a nonprofit called Getting Out and Staying Out (GOSO), on East 116th Street and Madison Avenue. Mark Goldsmith, Mr. G to his colleagues and to the young men he works with, founded GOSO after a life-changing visit to Rikers Island in 2003.

As a volunteer in the Principal for a Day program, Goldsmith, a retired business executive, had asked for the toughest high school in the city. They gave him Horizon Academy on Rikers. There he talked to inmates about what landed them in Rikers—peddling crack cocaine, illegal gun possession—and how that "work" differs from a normal job with a salary, benefits and advancement opportunities. Such a job, he told them, might break the cycle of getting out, getting arrested, and returning to Rikers again and again.

Out of that conversation and subsequent visits, GOSO was born. It now helps hundreds of young men a year, ages 16 to 24: some are incarcerated in Rikers or in upstate prisons; the balance, released from jail, are enrolled in programs that can lead to employment, a high school diploma, help getting into college.

Jackson and his colleagues at SAVE are in daily contact with a different, smaller group, 30 or 40, all from Johnson and Jefferson Houses. They range from mid-teens to mid-20s. All are at risk of engaging in violence; many have already done jail time. SAVE's street—level office is chock a block with flyers for educational programs, job fairs and boxes of healthy snacks.

My visit is part of a quest to better understand the life choices of GOSO's and SAVE's clients—some in gangs, others living on the streets—and to make whatever sense I can of the terrible violence these young men can wreak.

Four months earlier, I spent a good part of December 2017 at 100 Centre Street, Manhattan, in a trial that brought home the agonizing consequences—for victims, their families and for the perpetrator—of a single violent act in East Harlem. I was one of 12 jurors in that trial and thus, my vote helped determine its outcome.

On the wall behind Omar Jackson's desk is a white board that displays a scorecard, its numbers handwritten in erasable ink for daily updating. On the day of my visit it reads, referring to nearby Jefferson and Johnson Houses, "No shootings. 358 days."

CHAPTER 1

THE DICE GAME

In the early morning hours of June 7, 2007, five young men were playing dice in the courtyard of East River Houses, a New York City Housing Authority project in East Harlem between East 102nd and East 105th streets and between First Avenue and the FDR Drive. Three of the players were members of the Bloods gang and two were Crips. The two gangs were rivals for drug-selling territory; their interactions occasionally turned violent. But a truce, brokered by the mother of one of the gang leaders, seemed to have ushered in a period of calm. Hence the dice game.

The weather that early morning in New York was cool (59 degrees) and dry; the high that day would be 76. The area of the dice game was well-lit with flood lights illuminating that area of the courtyard in front of building 404. At a little past 4:30 A.M., one of the dice players, Alejandro Alvarez*, heard shots and leapt over a nearby retaining

---

*The names of the two eyewitnesses, Alvarez and Gabriel Washington, have been changed for their protection; both are the target of threats from gang members

wall to safety. When he raised his head, he recognized the shooter as his constant companion, the leader of a Bloods drug-selling crew called PIRU (pimps in red uniforms). PIRU's territory was an area of East River Houses below the main courtyard, near 102nd Street.

Alvarez was the right-hand man of this crew leader, whom he regarded as friend and protector. According to sworn testimony by Alvarez and another eyewitness, Gabriel Washington, the shooter then moved toward a red bench 50 feet from the dice players and continued firing.

He had apparently been aiming at Wyatt Rudolph, nicknamed Booga, the Crips leader from nearby Wilson Houses on the north side of East 105th Street; presumably the shooter was unaware (because he'd been in Kentucky for most of the previous six months), that a local Bloods-Crips truce was in effect. Instead of hitting Rudolph, who fled in the direction of 105th Street, one of his shots struck Manuel Sabater. Sabater, a fellow Blood, belonged to a second Bloods drug-selling crew, this one operating in the main courtyard in East River Houses and calling itself Sex Money Murder (SMM).

The shooter continued running toward and firing at Rudolph until it was clear his intended victim had gotten away. He came back to the dice players and, realizing that he had hit Sabater, then aimed his weapon, a 40-caliber semi-automatic pistol, at an 18-year-old named Joshua Agard. Agard, a three-and-a half-foot tall dwarf, was also a Crip and Wyatt Rudolph's right-hand man. Agard was well-liked and in fact had friends in both Bloods and Crips.

Washington, like Sabater a member of the Bloods/SMM crew, would testify that he'd been playing dice next to Agard until Sabater was shot. He bent to comfort Manny but was still close enough to hear Joshua Agard plead for his life. From a distance of no more than a few feet, the shooter then fired a succession of shots into Agard's torso and head. As Agard lay bleeding face down on the ground, this witness would say, the shooter pronounced the words, "Bloods up," as if announcing the score: Bloods one, Crips zero. Except that his tally omitted the second casualty, fellow Blood Manuel Sabater, whom he had also just killed. At the time of the shooting, Manuel Sabater, of Puerto Rican background, was 27. Joshua Agard, an African-American, was 18.

After multiple calls to 911 from East River residents, police were quickly on the scene. Ambulances took Agard and Sabater to local hospitals. Both were pronounced dead within minutes of their arrival.

CHAPTER 2

THE MOST SERIOUS CASE YOU COULD BE INVOLVED IN

On November 20, 2017, in room 1324 of 100 Centre Street, Manhattan, the presiding New York State Supreme Court judge, Michael Obus, is telling a chamber packed with 200 prospective jurors, "This is the most serious case you could be involved in." Pointing to the defendant, a 35-year-old named Abraham Cucuta, the judge explains that he is charged with the first degree murder of Manuel Sabater and Joshua Agard, a crime that occurred ten years earlier. The reasons for the long delay will become clear during trial. From my seat near the rear of the courtroom, it's impossible to see anything of the defendant except his close crew cut and a swath of his black and white checkered shirt as he listens to the judge. Obus says the trial will be in session Mondays, Tuesdays and Wednesdays, and estimates that it will last three weeks.

He asks those who are unable to serve because of the time commitment—or for any other reason—to raise their hands. A forest of hands sprouts; two-thirds of those in the room want no part of this case. Obus then asks those who *can* serve to raise their hands. All the others are excused.

I'm among that group of 60 or 70 who stay. Within minutes, the court clerk is spinning a large drum containing our juror identification cards. After each spin she lifts out a card. My name is called, along with the names of 17 others; we take our seats in the jury box, to be questioned by the judge, by the assistant district attorney (ADA) and senior trial counsel, Dafna Yoran, and by the defense attorney, Dawn Florio.

The questioning goes on for more than two hours. Do we have any predisposition for or against the police and the prosecution? Can we remain impartial until all the testimony has been concluded? Have any family members ever been convicted of a crime, have they been in gangs or sold drugs? Can we weigh the testimony of eyewitnesses, taking into account that they are receiving some benefit (reduced sentences in other cases) in exchange for their cooperation? By now it is after 4 P.M. The judge tells all 18 of us to return the next morning.

On Tuesday morning the courtroom is again full with not only the 60 or 70 from the previous day also but an influx of new prospective jurors. Of the 18 from yesterday, the clerk reads only four names; mine is the second.

I'm now juror number 2 in The People vs. Abraham Cucuta.

That afternoon and the next morning, the judge, prosecution and defense agree on the rest of the jurors, 12 in all, and four alternates. We're told to return next Monday for the start of trial.

For most of these two days of jury selection it's as if I'm looking at myself from outside, wondering what this person (me) is doing here. I didn't show up for jury duty to be on a trial; in fact, I specifically asked for November 20 because it was a short week, Thanksgiving week, and I assumed, wrongly, that there would be no major cases starting.

When the judge asked for hands of those who couldn't serve, why did my hands stay at my sides? The questioning offered another out. All I had to say, with false humility and lowered eyes, was sorry, I don't think I can be impartial. A few others do so, and it's their goodbye ticket. But not me. The person I'm looking at is telling himself, if you're ever going to do this—I've been called a half a dozen times and never been on a jury—this is the time and this is the case.

—⚏—

THE FOLLOWING Monday morning we wait in the corridor outside Room 1324 until a court officer brings us into the jurors' room, a narrow space with a large TV screen at one end and an old-fashioned blackboard, actually a green board, in the middle of the long interior wall. The blackboard comes complete with broken pieces of chalk and ancient erasers; I don't know if I've seen one of those since high school.

The opposite, outer wall, facing Centre Street, has large windows that look to be in permanent lockdown. There are radiators, a couple of window air-conditioners and standing on the floor, a water cooler. Usually one or two spare bottles sit next to the cooler. It's warm in this room and we drink a lot of water.

At the far end are two small bathrooms, men's and women's. A large rectangular table seats 12; four other chairs are squeezed in between the table and the walls.

We spend a lot of time here. Most of being a juror is waiting. We're told to be there at 9:45 each morning but often one or two jurors are late by an hour or more as the rest of us sit—and fume. Even if we all arrive by ten we may not get called into the courtroom till 11 or 11:15. There's lunch recess, there are often morning and afternoon breaks and after each of these we wait in the room. Four hours in court is a full day.

By the second day of trial I've settled on the best route to 100 Centre Street. The walk gives me time to clear my head, to put away lists of errands to do and phone calls to make, and to get ready for a day of work. Make no mistake, listening to the testimony in The People vs. Abraham Cucuta is work: tedious, exasperating, absorbing, horrifying, and ultimately momentous.

East River Houses, scene of the crime, is not that far from West 12th Street where I live. Nevertheless, its universe of gangs, drugs and violence, of 12 and 13-year-olds hanging out on the street and steering addicts to 15-year-olds who take the customers' money and hand over bags of crack cocaine, is an unknown world to me. Over the next several weeks, however, I'm immersed in it as I listen to days of testimony. The two key prosecution witnesses have lived this life, and what they have to show for it are years or decades in prison.

My route to court takes me down Sixth Avenue and across Washington Square Park with the Arch to my left. The central walkway of the park is lovely a little after 8 A.M. on a late November morning as I stride through a scattering of leaves lit golden by rising sun.

I turn into the passageway hard by NYU's Bobst Library, through Washington Square Village and east to

Lafayette and south, past the upscale shops and cafes of Noho and Soho.

As I walk I'm thinking about East Harlem, originally known as El Barrio, where the murders took place. Striding along Lafayette, passing through old immigrant neighborhoods where tenement buildings once housed my grandparents and their families, not to mention factories and garment sweat shops, reminds me again of how inexorably the city changes. The urban past is not so much swept away as eased, sometimes gradually, sometimes abruptly, into distant memory. Old-timers gazing at the window of a sleek clothing store or an emporium with a dozen different choices of coffee bean may have trouble remembering what once stood here: the vintage candy shop with the soda fountain, or the furniture store with sofas out on the sidewalk. Change is all around, and yet, what I'm hearing about the children growing up in East River Houses makes me wonder if such a transformation will ever happen there.

Lafayette merges into Centre; signs in Chinese begin to appear. And suddenly here is Canal Street, not yet gentrified, with the odors, urgency and rough garb of an older New York. Another couple of blocks bring me to 100 Centre, up the broad steps, through stiff glass doors to security. I empty phone, wallet, keys, spare change, jacket and backpack onto the conveyer belt, and step through the electronic gate for the final caress of the wand wielded by an unsmiling officer.

—⁂—

On a typical morning in the jurors' room, John, an alternate and professional singer, is doing the daily Times puzzle. Harvey, retired, is checking London stock prices on his iPad, looking for arbitrage opportunities (he used to manufacture clothing, and seems not to have any money worries, though he dresses in well-worn hoodies). Kristen, who works for a healthcare consulting firm, is on her laptop doing homework for her MBA studies at Fordham, while Sophia, a fifth grade English teacher, is using her laptop for lesson planning or correcting student work. Christen, an architect, is sketching on ruled paper: designs for a private house upstate, he tells me.

Emily, a real estate broker with Compass, is talking to her assistant at the office—inquiries, listings, deals; she works hard and apparently has the results to show for it. Nakia, an alternate, talks constantly, theatrically, often to Joselina, our lone Hispanic female.

Marc (finance, between jobs), Miguel (Hispanic, slight of build, sweet-tempered, dark-complexioned, retired), Melissa (state employee, alternate), Olivia (as juror number 1 she is automatically named forewoman) and I are the quiet ones. Daniel, also an alternate and only in his 20s, is sometimes talkative and sometimes silent; he works nights at the Penn Station McDonalds and arrives pasty-faced and sleep-deprived.

Sam, in his mid-30s, hyperkinetic and expressive, stirs things up; he's loud and loves to laugh. He's in sales with a legal publisher. The joking and repartee keep our minds off the trial, which we are not supposed to discuss but which we can't stop thinking about.

This business of not discussing the trial is hard. Judge Obus offers this admonition at the start and at the end of every session. He greets us that first Monday by saying "Ladies and gentlemen, thank you very much," and this too he repeats every time we arrive or leave, even after a 15-minute bathroom break. He is courtesy personified.

My fellow jurors are unanimous in their praise of Obus. Very impressive, intelligent, fair, patient, an outstanding professional, they say and then, in the ultimate encomium, "like a TV judge"—the very model of calm, decorum and fairness.

Michael Obus, 70, has been on the bench since 1986, a New York State Supreme Court justice since 1993. He has a thin face with a prominent nose. His dark hair, now graying, is mostly full. Because we always see him seated, I can only guess how tall he is. Five-nine, I'm thinking, with little excess weight; later I learn that he plays men's senior basketball. He speaks precisely but is never pedantic, never ill-tempered. Even when one of the lawyers—usually Florio—tries his and the jurors' patience, he does not yield to irritation.

His maxims, repeated over and over, seem to come from his very core. The defendant is presumed innocent until the end of the trial. Keep an open mind; refrain from forming opinions until all the testimony has been heard. Do not discuss the case with anyone, including among yourselves. Do not read about the case, nor use the Internet to look up anything about the case, nor visit the scene of the crime. Do not talk to or even say hello to the lawyers. If anyone attempts to talk to you, report it promptly to a court officer.

That first morning he explains that the opening statements we are about to hear are not evidence but arguments. Our decision is to be based on testimony and evidence, nothing else. We jurors are the sole judges of this evidence; no one else's opinion counts. And then it begins.

CHAPTER 3

THE TRIAL

Dafna Yoran's second chair, assistant DA James Lynch, delivers the prosecution's opening statement. He describes two gangs, Bloods and Crips; two housing projects, East River and Wilson; two groups of Bloods (PIRU and Sex Money Murder), each in a different area of East River but competing for drug sales. He tells us about shootings, about the truce between Bloods and Crips. And he recounts, step by step, the prosecution's version of the crime: the path the shooter took, the number of shots he fired, the triumphant words he spoke after executing Agard.

He also gives us the nicknames, standard for anyone in a gang or selling drugs. Cucuta, the defendant, is Holiday; his associate, Alejandro Alvarez, a main prosecution witness, is Double A; the head of SMM, Michael Kearse, is Shyce. (His right-hand man, Gabriel Washington, the other key prosecution witness, is Gabes.) As for the two victims, Joshua Agard is Josh (or Midget), while Manuel

Sabater is Manny Mo. Wyatt Rudolph, head of the Crips in Wilson Houses, is Booga. The associates, bit players or witnesses also have nicknames: Double R, Tripp, Banner, Mez.

After the onslaught of names and events in Lynch's statement, I'm thoroughly confused.

Dawn Florio's opening statement for the defense could not be more different. Where Lynch offers facts, or rather, the prosecution's version of the facts, she makes an emotional plea to us to be skeptical and to doubt. The defendant, she shouts, standing close to the jury, is presumed innocent now and at every moment of the trial. Nothing compels him to testify, or requires the defense to offer even a single witness. And if he doesn't testify, and if the defense presents no witnesses, he is still entitled to the presumption of innocence. It's up to the prosecution to provide its case beyond a reasonable doubt.

Florio is a large woman, tall, markedly overweight. Her dyed blond hair is almost white under the courtroom lights, her long painted nails an object of discussion for the female jurors. Her back is bent at what looks like a 20-degree angle, and as she hobbles back and forth between the defense table and the stance she takes near the jury box, we can't help imagining her physical discomfort and feeling sympathy for her and for the sales job she has taken on.

Doubt is what she is selling us. The two eyewitnesses, she points out, are convicted felons testifying under cooperation agreements, meaning they're getting something in exchange for their testimony. Both were drinking heavily the night of the murder. Both, she claims, were also smoking PCP (angel dust) up until the time of the shooting (One, Double A, will readily admit smoking PCP that night; the other, Gabes denies ever smoking PCP, though he does smoke marijuana.) Angel dust, she insists, is a hallucinogen; it alters reality; it puts the smoker outside himself, making him see and hear things that are not there.

Another source of doubt is the absence of any physical evidence linking the defendant to the crime scene. The prosecution concedes this; Florio hammers away at it. It's her strongest point. No gun; the type of weapon, a 40-caliber semi-automatic, was identified from cartridge casings but the actual gun was never found. No security camera footage with his image. No fingerprints or DNA of the defendant on anything at the scene. No hair or fibers or articles of clothing showing he was there. In the TV world, maybe the crackerjack technicians of NCIS Miami could have found something but the NYPD, its patrolmen, detectives, crime scene techs and lab personnel came up empty.

It's already clear to us from Florio's statement that Abraham Cucuta will not be taking the stand and exposing himself to cross-examination by the prosecution. Nor does she promise any alibi, no girlfriend or buddy or relative who will say the defendant was with me between 4:15 and 4:45 that morning, and thus could not have been murdering two young men rolling dice in the East River Houses courtyard.

To us, therefore, Abraham Cucuta is and will remain a mystery man for the entire trial. When he's not in court is he at liberty or in prison? At what age did he join the Bloods? How many times has he been arrested and convicted? Have any of those arrests involved violence? We are permitted no answers to these questions; we can't even ask them. For all we know of his past, Cucuta has never fired a weapon more dangerous than a cap gun.

We see him every day at the defense table in his checkered shirt. He sometimes looks bored, or annoyed at a witness, but never stunned or stricken; he doesn't smile, groan or shake his head. He often takes notes on a pad of lined paper; at times he fills an entire sheet. When Florio walks to the defense table in the middle of one of her cross examinations, they lean toward each other and exchange a few words. The only emotion he ever displays comes near the very end of the trial, after Florio finishes her closing statement. A spontaneous grin lights up his features. Defendant and lawyer touch hands, either a high-five or a fist-bump, I can't see which. Great job, he's telling her,

Over the course of the next three weeks the prosecution presents a couple of dozen witnesses. The location and approximate time of the murders are established by the testimony of police officers and 911 operators. A map shows the layout of East River Houses with its ten buildings, courtyard, parking areas, basketball court. Witnesses point to photographs to indicate where the bodies of Manny and Josh fell and those photos show the shocking extent of the blood stains (mostly from Josh's body) in the area—it looks as if most of the contents of a can of red paint had spilled onto the cement. Exhibits consisting of photographs, names and nicknames, and later, cellphone numbers, identify the main characters of the drama: Holiday, Booga, Manny Mo, Double A, Josh, Gabes, Shyce.

Crime scene investigators, police lab technicians and ballistics and DNA experts explain their efforts to collect evidence and from it, identify who was at the scene.

(Some evidence was destroyed in the Sandy storm, and from what remained there was little to learn. Alejandro Alvarez's fingerprints on a beer bottle did, however, confirm his account of being in the courtyard that morning.) Detectives and an assistant district attorney recount what gang members told them in the weeks after the shootings. In those interviews both Washington and Alvarez identified Cucuta as the shooter back in 2007; neither was then willing to testify.

Police witnesses also document how cellphones were collected from various participants in the events of June 7, 2007; the cellphones themselves, along with detailed telephone company logs of calls, are introduced into evidence. An outside expert explains how cellphone calls are routed to cell towers, and what call records can tell us about the location from which a specific call was made.

At the time it's unclear that they mean, these call logs and maps of nearby cellphone towers. As juror number 2, I sit in the second chair of the first row of the jury box, looking at and listening to witnesses maybe a dozen feet away. The video screen on which these images are projected is every bit as close. But in the course of a day we hear a tremendous amount of detail, some of it repetitive, some clearly extraneous. Witnesses don't always speak clearly; at times my attention wanders. And though I'm taking notes, the judge forbids us to remove those notes from the jury box to review them at the end of each day, making it difficult to fix details in the mind.

By trial's end, however, cellphone logs and maps will emerge as a crucial key to the central puzzle: who was in the courtyard of East River Houses before, during and after the murders.

It's not until December 12, near the end of the prosecution case, that the deputy chief medical examiner, Dr. Jason Graham, takes the stand to introduce autopsy photos of the bodies of Manuel Sabater and Joshua Agard. These are hard to look at, especially those of Josh, showing the grievous damage done to his body by execution-style shots fired at close range.

The most gruesome and infuriating photo is a close-up showing the bloody, mangled tip of Josh's pinkie, almost severed from the base of the finger—a wound, says Dr. Graham, "consistent with" the victim's raising his hand as if to ward off a bullet being fired down into his skull.

That night I write these words: "I kept seeing those photos in my mind as I walked home, and the last thing I felt like doing was showing up at a holiday party tonight to celebrate the lighting of the Hanukkah candles. But there was this benefit of recalling those images. Two young people are dead, brutally murdered and while we owe the defendant a fair trial, we also have an obligation to the memory of (and families of) Manny and Josh to see that justice is done."

CHAPTER 4

GABRIEL WASHINGTON

On November 28, the second full day of trial, Yoran calls Gabriel Washington as a witness. Washington, 35, has been arrested numerous times; in another, unrelated case, he faces a possible sentence of 25 years to life for murder in the second degree (his cooperation agreement gives him a reduction to 18 years flat). He is here now as one of two eyewitnesses to the murders.

In direct examination by prosecutors, Washington testifies:

That he grew up in Building 425 in Wilson Houses, on the north side of East 105th Street, opposite East River Houses.

That he lived there with his father and his paternal grandmother, while his mother and his maternal grandmother lived across the street in Building 410 of East River Houses.

That in 1994, when he was 12, his parents died within a few months of each other, his mother of pneumonia, his father of a stroke.

That shortly thereafter, he dropped out of school and took to the streets to sell crack cocaine with Manny Sabater, two years older. They'd known each other since they were young children.

"I would be outside cutting school," Gabriel testifies, "and he was like, 'You want to make some money? Let's go.' . . . And I was hanging with him," selling crack cocaine.

That in August 1997, at 15, he was arrested for sale of a controlled substance and after failing an ATD (alternatives to detention) school, spent a few months at Spofford Juvenile Detention Center, then was sent upstate to Pius 12, a residential facility for juvenile offenders. Several months later, "I went AWOL." He put a dummy in the bed in his cell to fool the guards, snuck out, walked to Poughkeepsie, then begged money for a train ticket back to Manhattan.

Back at Wilson Houses, "I'd meet up with Manny, go to East River and sell drugs."

That in 1997 he joined the Bloods, a gang whose color is red and whose members pledge to help one another and stick together in case of violence. His initiation?

"I had to 'take a plate,'" i.e., cut a rival gang member. He went up to a Latin Kings gang member (identified by the colors he was wearing) and slashed his face with a razor.

By now I'm sitting with my eyes trained on Gabriel Washington's clean-shaven face, listening to every word and immersing myself in the reality of what he is saying. Articulate and intelligent, he moved from one bad decision to another—almost as if he'd boarded a train destined for derailment, a train that never made a stop where he could get off.

Of course I know there are kids like Gabriel, but I've never met any. Between the ages of 12 and 15 my older son pursued the trumpet as avidly as Gabriel Washington peddled crack cocaine. He'd take the train by himself to Philadelphia for lessons with a highly regarded teacher of jazz improvisation. In his attic bedroom he practiced incessantly.

At the same age, my younger son fell in love with the outdoors. With teen hiking groups he conquered peaks in Colorado and Washington State, including Mt. Rainier. At 15, by himself, he hiked the Long Trail in Vermont, 272 miles from Massachusetts to Canada.

Both boys were good students. Sometimes they stayed out too late, violating curfew. At times they weren't truthful about where they'd been and what they'd done. At least twice, little packets of marijuana would slip out of the pants they threw into the washing machine. I can't remember if they broke windows playing ball; I don't know if they ever shoplifted anything. For sure neither was ever arrested.

For Gabriel Washington, however, the train kept rolling.

He testifies that he married a girlfriend with whom he has six children, the oldest a girl of 20.

That in December 1998 (at 16) he was arrested for armed robbery, pled guilty and served two years in prison. (The crime: he and several others got his sister to lure some boys to a rendezvous; they surrounded them, brandished knives and stole their jackets.)

That when released he broke parole, was sent back to jail and served another 18 months.

That after release in December 2002, "I went back to my old tricks, selling drugs"—this time by himself because his buddy Manny was in jail. Arrested once again for possession of crack cocaine, he pled guilty to a misdemeanor and served six months.

That when he got out in 2005, he began hanging out with a Bloods drug-selling crew in East River, headed by Shyce (Michael Kearse). This is the crew that calls itself Sex Money Murder. Shyce ranked very high in the Bloods ("godfather") and because he vouched for Gabriel, Gabriel was readmitted to the gang. (He'd been expelled from the Bloods while jailed for armed robbery, because he'd refused to attack someone in prison.)

That he became Shyce's right-hand man.

The meaning of right-hand man? "Whenever you seen one you seen the other. If you seen Shyce you seen me. If you seen me you seen Shyce."

That at this time, SMM's sale of crack cocaine was becoming increasingly lucrative; Gabriel was making anywhere from a couple of hundred to a thousand dollars a day.

That when he was arrested yet again in February 2007 for selling drugs to an undercover cop, he lied about his actions. In a major stroke of luck, he was allowed to cop a plea to possession.

At this point in the saga of Gabriel Washington—on the street since age 11 or 12, four arrests on drug selling and armed robbery charges (twice giving false names when arrested), multiple parole violations, at least six years in jail—it is late spring of 2007. He is 25 years old.

The assistant DA now asks, "In June 2007 did you witness a murder?"

"Yes."

Who was murdered?

"Manny and Josh."

"Did you talk to the police and tell them what you saw?"

"Yes."

"Were you willing to testify?"

"No."

Having established this fact, the prosecutors then pose a series of questions about the events of Gabriel Washington's life after June 2007: more arrests, more charges, more jail time, a serious rift with Shyce (Michael Kearse).

Shyce had put up bail after one of Washington's arrests, enabling him to stay out of jail until trial. Then, two and a half months after the June 7th murders, cops stopped Gabriel coming out of building 440 in East River and threatened to arrest him for trespassing. He told them what apartment he'd come from. When the cops rang the bell and a woman opened the door, the cops spotted Shyce—with a huge quantity of drugs. Shyce was sentenced to nine years in prison. By then he'd retracted the bail money he'd put up for Gabriel and Gabriel, too, wound up back in prison.

Upon release in 2010, Gabriel resumed selling drugs, first on his own; then he went into business with two guys from Brooklyn to sell drugs in Brooklyn and in Manhattan. In December 2011, after concocting a plan with Gabriel to rob a marijuana dealer in East River, the other two wound up confronting the supposed dealer (they actually had the wrong man) and shot him to death. Though Gabriel was not there when shots were fired, he was charged with felony murder; he faces a maximum sentence of 25 years to life.

He signed a cooperation agreement. In exchange for his testimony against his associates, and his agreement to testify about any and all other crimes that he knows about, the DA's office will reduce the charge to manslaughter in the first degree and recommend a sentence of 18 years flat. If Gabriel upholds his agreement and if the judge approves the DA's recommended sentence, he will still be in prison until his early to mid-50s.

It's as a result of that cooperation agreement, signed when Gabriel was facing a possible life sentence in an unrelated case, that he is on the stand now.

He's not the only one from East River Houses in the courtroom today. His one-time mentor, Shyce, and several other gang members from the projects are midway back in the spectators' section, staring at Gabriel as if daring him to proceed. The code for Blood gang members is clear: you never cooperate with police and prosecutors against a fellow Blood.

And if you do? the prosecutor asks.

"Snitches get stitches," Gabriel answers. Since this trial began, there've been Facebook posts from gang members threatening him.

Nevertheless, on November 28, 2017, under direct examination and after testifying about all the events of his truncated childhood and his criminal history, Gabriel begins to recount in detail the events of June 6 and June 7, 2007.

On June 6 Gabriel and Manny spent a good part of the day with Shyce, who had a birthday coming up and decided to treat himself to some clothes. The three of them went shopping in midtown, including the Gucci store on Fifth Avenue

Gucci? I see some of my fellow jurors raise an eyebrow and after a second I think, Why not? If Gabriel was pulling down a thousand dollars on a good day, maybe

Shyce, a Bloods godfather and area bigshot, was making twice that.

That evening they were in the East River courtyard with other SMM crew members, drinking and smoking PCP. (Gabriel drank and smoked weed but insists he never smoked PCP, not that night or any other night.) Shyce had romantic plans; he left to meet a woman at a hotel in the Bronx. Gabriel and Manny remained in the courtyard. A number of others, including Holiday (Cucuta), Double A (Alejandro Alvarez) and Booga (Wyatt Rudoph), the Crips crew leader, were also in the courtyard that evening. A dice game started; Booga was playing, along with Double A. Gabriel joined the game.

He testifies that at some point Holiday and Double A came back from buying food and beer and offered beer to the others. Booga, apparently sensing danger, chirped Josh on his phone and asked him to join him at the game and to bring a gun. The presence of this gun tucked into Josh's waistband was itemized on the autopsy report. Holiday sat by himself at a concrete bench. He wanted no part of the dice game; he was eating, watching and smoking PCP.

"I took a Corona, Manny took one," Gabriel remembers. He limited himself to one Corona "because I was the lookout for Manny," who was carrying money from drug sales that day. (This too was confirmed by the discovery, during the autopsy, of a plastic bag in his rectum containing money and drugs.) By now it was after 4 A.M.

Then Holiday left by himself, Gabriel says. "He walked off toward the parking lot at 103rd Street."

How long was he gone? the ADA asks.

"A few minutes."

Can you tell us what happened then?

"A few minutes go by. He comes back. I'm down on the floor picking up the dice. The first two shots ring out. I look up and see Holiday running in my direction."

By this time Gabriel was kneeling on one knee because Manny was on the floor, shot. He saw Holiday running past him in pursuit of Booga, but Booga got away. Gabriel was comforting Manny, telling him to stay down. Manny couldn't speak, there was blood coming out of his mouth. Now Holiday was coming toward the dice players and Josh was pleading with Gabriel, "'Yo, your homie's coming back. Yo, please don't let him kill me.'"

Gabriel, still trying to keep Manny responsive, answered, "You're all right, you're good." But Josh kept repeating, he's coming, he's coming. When Holiday reached the scene of the dice game he saw Manny on the floor, shot.

"He looks down and I look up to him and I'm like, Yo, what the fuck are you doing? And he sees Josh there and he just started firing. Shot Josh and he just kept shooting."

How close were you to Josh?

"Josh was a foot away. He fell face down. I just recall seeing his little body bouncing off the concrete."

How many shots did Holiday fire?

"Multiple times. Probably about eight."

Did Holiday say anything?

"Yes, he said, 'Bloods up.'"

What does that mean?

"It means like Bloods win, Bloods won the war."

In response to Yoran's questions, Gabriel says that while playing dice he was facing in the direction of the basketball court, the direction Holiday came from. That there was plenty of light from two floodlights, otherwise they couldn't have seen the dice. That Holiday was carrying a big gun, a semi-automatic. That he saw Holiday running and firing at Booga, saw sparks from the gun, saw cartridge casings fall to the ground.

As Gabriel recounts this scene, I am not looking at the defendant, the judge, my fellow jurors. I am intent only on the witness speaking into the microphone. I'm not thinking that the man who's speaking is a career criminal, tough enough to slash the face of a Latin Kings member, bold enough to escape from detention, hardened enough to survive years in prison. What I'm hearing are the words of someone traumatized by the merciless assassination he's just witnessed. In all his years as a gang member, he'd never seen anyone shot and killed. When the shots struck Joshua Agard's neck and head, Gabriel recalls, he saw the puff of smoke coming from his neck. No doubt he could still hear the echo of Josh's plea: "Please don't let your homie kill me."

CHAPTER 5

ALEJANDRO ALVAREZ

If Gabriel Washington is the only sworn eyewitness to the shooting on June 7, 2007, the prosecution will have a very tough case to make. Yes, his testimony is riveting. But when he steps down from the witness chair, the admonition of Judge Obus is front and center in my mind: Refrain from forming an opinion until you've heard all the evidence.

Common sense (and hundreds of detective novels) tell me that a single eyewitness is suspect. The witness may mis-identify a suspect for any number of reasons: poor eyesight, poor visibility (bad weather, insufficient light), his or her physical distance from the crime, impermissible coaching by police. In the worst case, the witness may lie out of malice toward the defendant or a desire to shift blame from himself to that defendant.

The rule of thumb that a single witness should not be relied upon goes back thousands of years. The Book of Deuteronomy in the Old Testament sets down an unambiguous law in Chapter 19, verse 15: "A single witness may not validate against a person any guilt or blame for any offense that may be committed; a case can be valid only on the testimony of two witnesses or three."

And in fact the prosecution, which knew of Gabriel's cooperation agreement from another case back in 2012, did not move to indict Abraham Cucuta until a second witness agreed to testify under a cooperation agreement signed in 2016.

That second witness, Alejandro Alvarez, takes the stand on Tuesday, December 5. It is quickly apparent that his personal story is even more wrenching than Gabriel's.

At the time he raises his hand and swears to tell the whole truth, Alejandro is 33 years old. He takes his seat and faces ADA James Lynch, who stands perhaps 25 feet away. From my place in the jury box, I'm even closer to Alvarez. I see a man whose face bears the accumulation of decades of loneliness and humiliation, of being bullied, of constantly running away, of drug addiction—and of criminal acts and their consequences. There is something vulnerable, almost tender about Alejandro; he displays none of Gabriel Washington's bravado. In pushing back against Dawn Florio's aggressive cross-examination, Gabriel was combative in a way that Alejandro cannot be.

Lynch first establishes that Alejandro grew up in Building 430 of East River Houses (East 105th Street), along with his mother, father, a younger sister and later, a younger brother. Now he asks, What was your relationship with your mother?

She was a drug addict, Alejandro replies. She used to take us to different crack houses.

Did you see your mother use drugs?

Yes. We used to be in crack houses when she was smoking crack cocaine. She would give me a water pistol to shoot out the window to amuse myself.

Was there a time when your mother left the family?

Yes, when I was six. My father put her out. He thought it wasn't healthy for us to be with her when she was high on crack.

Under questioning, Alejandro explains that his father worked weekends, and until very late at night, in after-hours clubs. Sometimes he was gone for two or three days, leaving six-year-old Alejandro to watch his younger siblings. The instructions were: Don't answer the phone, don't open the door. His father left food for the children as well as food stamps; in those days they were paper, not the debit-type cards of today, and when the food ran out, Alejandro, as the adult, went to the grocery store to buy more.

Was there a time when you got injured?

Yes. Alejandro relates that one of the games he and his siblings played was to pour water on the floor to make a water slide. Once he slid, slipped onto broken glass and tore a gash in his leg from the ankle to the knee. The wound bled profusely.

What happened then?

"I took a towel, wrapped my leg up as best I could, and my little sister and brother laid on it that night hoping that I didn't pass away, hoping I wasn't going to die."

Did you ever go to the hospital?

No.

Eventually, Alejandro recounts, his father began dating a woman who moved in with them. Alejandro was then seven or eight. He was able to give up some of his adult chores, like translating for his father (born in Cuba and speaking no English) at doctors' appointments.

"I became a child for a while," he says.

However, this newcomer to the family was, in Alejandro's words "very dominant—the mean stepmother," who insisted on discipline and meted out punishment. She played favorites, her favorite being Alejandro's younger brother. Often she berated Alejandro for his physical appearance.

"I was very fat," he explains. "I wasn't good enough to go play basketball or football with the other kids."

Where did you go to school?

PS 146 on First Avenue and East 106th Street.

What was school like?

"I was picked on, I was called fat boy because of my weight. I didn't fight back."

Things got no better at Junior High School 117 on East 109th Street. He never had good clothes at a time when it became cool to have the right clothes, the right sneakers.

As for life in East River, "I was an outcast, I was chased, I was an easy target" for other kids. At age 12 he was jumped and robbed at knife point. He had no uncle or cousins to stand up for him. He never told his father about these experiences.

As a result of the treatment he endured, "I used to run away a lot."

In the early grades of elementary school he once ran away after recess and stayed out on the streets until a cop found him after midnight and brought him home. In the fifth grade he ran away for three months.

Why did you run away?"

"It was very uncomfortable at home, outside I couldn't play in a park. I was always in some type of stress."

How did you survive?

Here Alejandro's story becomes a litany of jumbled but vivid memories. He stayed briefly at Covenant House, where he had a bed and could shower but where he did not feel safe (his bag was stolen). He hung out near Times Square, on Eighth Avenue and stole from tourists—bags, watches. Sometimes prostitutes befriended him and let him sleep in a nearby hotel they frequented. Sometimes he slept on trains. Eventually, at age 10 or 11, he got picked up by the cops on a PINS (person in need of supervision) warrant sought by his father, A family court judge sent him to a group home on Staten Island. That was fun for a while, Alejandro says, until another kid hit him in the face with a padlock. He ran away and for a time, returned home.

Soon he was back on the streets, smoking weed, selling drugs with older guys, staying up one or two nights at a time, sleeping on trains. Eventually the effects of marijuana took a toll. Feeling unwell, he walked to Metropolitan Hospital on First Avenue and East 97th Street, and, after shouting at a guard there, was taken to a mental hospital. There he stayed two, two and a half months. He was comfortable, well fed, had games to play, people to talk to. At one point, however, he started screaming while in a group session. Attendants were on the verge of giving him a shot, holding him down, when his stepmother walked in and put a stop to the injection.

Did you attend high school, the prosecutor asks.

Yes, Murray Bergtraum in downtown Manhattan, but here too he ran away after only two months. He spent three or four months with his grandmother in Florida, where he got arrested for shoplifting and then it was back to Manhattan, to Seward Park High School. This time he ran away after a month and a half. At age 15 and a half he was arrested for robbery and as a juvenile, was sent to Spofford and then to a drug treatment program on Staten Island. When they kicked him out for arguing, he was placed in another facility in the Bronx and then got a break. After pleading guilty, he received an unconditional discharge because he agreed to enlist in the army.

I look at my watch. Alejandro has been on the stand for a couple of hours and it's as if we've heard every page of *Oliver Twist* read aloud. And yet in his story he is barely 17 years old. There is no Fagin or Bill Sikes in Alejandro Alvarez's tale, no single villain who ensnares children and sends them into the streets to beg and steal. The neighborhood, the decrepit NYCHA project of East River Houses, the streets, the revolving door of the criminal justice system, the failing schools and perhaps most of all, the family or lack thereof—are these the villains? Do we blame forces beyond the control of a six-year-old, then a ten-year old, now a 17-year old, or do we say, No, he had choices, you always have choices.

I look right and left at my fellow jurors. Some of us are open-mouthed at this ordeal of childhood and now teenage misery. Can it be that the U.S. Army will be the salvation of this troubled young person? Can anyone with such a background be a credible witness to a murder?

At Fort Hamilton Alejandro passed all the written tests for army induction but failed the physical because he was overweight. Told to lose 25 to 30 pounds prior to enlistment, he began training with the recruiter, jogging, changing his diet. He got a job at the White Castle on First Avenue and 104th Street: cleanup crew, cashier, working on the grill.

Why did you stop? ADA Lynch asks.

Money. Years earlier Alejandro had been awarded $17,000 from a biking injury; the agreement called for the money to be paid out only when he turned 18. June 2, 2002 was his 18th birthday. Why work when you suddenly come into a fortune? And why enlist?

One day Alejandro walked into East River with bags of new clothes.

"I went from unpopular to popular. I came to East River and all of a sudden people were greeting me. They finally saw me for the first time."

Among his new friends was a young man nicknamed Holiday: Abraham Cucuta. Alejandro started hanging out with Holiday and with Holiday's girlfriend, Betzy.

In late September 2002, a friend brought a stolen car around; he got in and drove it. Cops arrested him. As an adult he faced a serious charge: grand larceny of a motor vehicle.

Were you incarcerated? the prosecutor asks

Yes, in Rikers Island.

How was that?

Like a nightmare come true, Alejandro says. But miraculously, he found a guardian angel: Abraham Cucuta was also imprisoned at Rikers.

"I ran into Holiday and he looked after me. He told everyone I was a good guy. He got me food, clothes, things I couldn't get for myself. I wasn't tough. I was still overweight."

How did you feel about Holiday?

What he did, says Alejandro, "was the ultimate thing. He became everything to me."

After six months in Rikers, Alejandro pled guilty and received five years' probation. He agreed to report to a supervisor, refrain from alcohol and drugs, observe a curfew. Once again he failed the test. He broke curfew, got sent to Phoenix House for 18 months of drug rehab, was dismissed for bad behavior, returned to East River and began selling crack cocaine on the corner of First Avenue and East 105th Street. The economics were simple: the bosses gave him $150 worth of crack, he sold it and gave them back $100. He could make a couple of hundred dollars a day.

Between 2005 and 2016, according to Alejandro's testimony, his life was a series of ups and downs, but the downs predominated, including a new low: addiction.

These long years include:

A few respectable jobs, Starbucks and a florist's shop in 2005–2006; a seafood restaurant and a cellphone store in 2011–2013. These jobs never lasted long. He got into arguments, quit, stole money from the restaurant when making takeout deliveries.

Selling drugs with his new mentor, Abraham Cucuta, who inducted him into the Bloods on his personal say-so, sparing Alejandro any painful initiation.

Keeping a stash of guns for the PIRU crew in a room he rented in a nearby project.

Fathering a child with a girlfriend who moved down south and refused to let him spend any time with his son.

Becoming a heavy user of angel dust, every day smoking $50 to $100 worth of cigarettes coated with PCP, a known hallucinogenic that can distort reality. Later, Dawn Florio will harp on the effects of PCP in her cross-examination, trying to get him to say he was hallucinating about what he saw on June 7, 2007. Alejandro insists both he and Holiday could function while smoking dust. It slowed me down, gave me the confidence to talk to girls, carry guns, he says.

More arrests: in December 2006 for sale of a controlled substance; in October 2014 on a similar charge, which led to incarceration in Rikers, the breaking of rules and a 17-day stay in "the box," solitary confinement, a punishment he was determined never to undergo again.

Taking up with a girlfriend who was addicted to crack and got Alejandro to smoke it, with disastrous results—"the worst decision I could have ever made," he testifies. In the years 2011 to 2013 he was smoking every day, desperate for a high that lasted ten seconds but that led to heightened sexual pleasure. In the grip of addiction he stole whatever and from whomever he could: money from takeout deliveries, $5,000 from a woman he agreed to marry so she could remain in the country legally. The deal was $5,000 up front and another $5,000 when the marriage and paperwork were complete. After the first payment he took off, forfeiting the balance.

More parole violations, more dropping out of mandated drug treatment programs.

Finally, facing a sentence of two to 12 years after the 2014 arrest, Alejandro did something he had steadfastly refused to do: agree to testify in court. In 2015 his lawyer contacted ADA David O'Keefe, who interviewed him back in 2007, to say he was now willing to take the stand.

By this time the Cucuta case was in the hands of Dafna Yoran and in August 2016 Alejandro Alvarez signed a cooperation agreement. In exchange for testifying truthfully about every crime he has ever witnessed or committed, whether or not there was an arrest, and refraining from any unlawful behavior, the DA's office agreed to recommend to the court a sentence of two years in prison and 18 months in a residential drug treatment program.

Since he has already served 22 months, if the judge accepts the recommendation he will be effectively liberated from jail.

Is there any further benefit to you, Lynch now asks.

Yes. The DA's office will furnish him with a sum of money to allow him to relocate out of New York and to put down a security deposit on a rental apartment.

Could you stay in New York?

No, because "what I'm doing is treason" in the eyes of former gang associates. (Later, under cross-examination, Alejandro will testify that his change of heart was the result of his finding God and realizing that the gang code he had previously honored was "false principles.")

Having led Alejandro Alvarez through an account of his life from age six through age 31, ADA Lynch now turns to the events of June 6 and 7, 2007.

He asks about Bloods-Crips tension in the spring of 2007, and Alejandro relates what he knows: that Tripp, a PIRU crew leader, had slapped Joshua Agard; that in retaliation Booga had shot at Tripp and Alejandro; that eventually Booga's mother Charlett came to East River Houses and demanded that members of both gangs make peace, insisting that if anyone shot her son, she would see that he spent the rest of his life in jail. An uneasy truce took hold.

June 6 was a busy day, Alejandro recounts. He was in court to plead guilty on the December 2006 arrest. That afternoon and evening he and other PIRU members hung out with an associate on the West Side; later they moved to the East Harlem apartment of a woman named Dolores, nicknamed Lola, where they drank, smoked PCP and assembled packets of crack cocaine for sale. Later that evening the two of them, other PIRU members, Shyce and his associates from Sex Money Murder were all hanging out in the East River courtyard. Various Crips, including Booga, were on the other side of the courtyard.

There was an incident in the courtyard: a girl from the Crips gang rode a bike back and forth in the courtyard and taunted some of the Bloods, calling them slobs.

Lynch asks, what was Holiday's reaction?

He was pissed, Alejandro recalls; angry at Shyce, presumably for allowing this disrespect in his territory, angry, too, at the presence of Booga and other Crips in the courtyard.

Nevertheless, Alejandro and Holiday walked over to a group of dice players and Alejandro joined the game.

"I love gambling," he explains, "I never walk by a dice game" without joining in. It didn't bother him that Booga was one of the dice players.

Did Holiday roll dice?

No, he stood to one side and watched.

At some point, Alejandro testifies, he and Holiday left to buy food and six-packs of Corona. On their return, they offered beers to the others.

Holiday sat by himself on a bench, eating, while Alejandro resumed rolling dice with Booga, Gabriel, Josh (who had joined the game) and Manny, all five of them crouching down, shoulder to shoulder, looking at the dice.

While playing dice were you watching Holiday?

No.

What happened next?

Manny had just rolled a point. It was Alejandro's turn. He heard a gunshot, jumped over the low wall and lay on the grass. He stuck his head up and saw Holiday with two hands on a gun, shooting. He was firing at Booga but didn't hit him.

What did you see first?

Holiday shooting.

What next?

Manny on the floor.

Didn't drinking and smoking PCP affect your perception?

"No, fear sobers you up."

How did you recognize Holiday?

"I knew his profile, I knew his walk."

What did he have in his hand?

A black automatic pistol.

Alejandro testifies that Holiday continued firing, that after Booga ran out of East River Houses, Holiday walked back to the dice players, pistol in his hand. Manny was down, shot, and Alejandro could hear Gabriel talking to him.

How far were you from Holiday and Manny?

About ten feet.

What happened next?

Holiday shot down at Josh. After Josh was already down, Holiday fired down at least three more times.

"I saw the bullets go into Josh. I saw the burn marks in Josh's shirt. I saw his white shirt turn red."

After the shootings, Alejandro testifies, Holiday walked across the basketball court to building 446. Alejandro followed.

"I lived there, it was my building," he explains.

In the lobby of the building he saw Holiday hand the gun, a 40-caliber pistol, to a man called Banner. He saw Holiday put his sweater, shirt and hat in the incinerator.

What did you do next?

"I had to go, no question. My best friend had just shot two people." After all, others might assume that he, Alejandro, was also implicated in the murders.

He quickly packed a bag, walked out of 446 toward 105th Street and caught a cab. He stayed at a girlfriend's house for a few days, then moved in with his sister in the Bronx.

What did you do in the cab?

"Shyce called up, threatening me. He said, 'You're a dead man. I promise I'm going to kill you and your entire family.'"

Alejandro also called Holiday from the cab and later that day they spoke again.

"He said he was going to Kentucky. He didn't have to say why."

On June 27, 2007, when he was at 100 Centre Street for a court appearance, Alejandro was approached and questioned by Detective Billy Dunn of the 23rd Precinct.

At first, "I didn't tell the truth" about what I knew, Alejandro testifies. But the questioning continued and eventually he admitted to having witnessed the shooting.

Did you tell them who did the shooting?

Yes.

What part did you not tell them about?

About continuing to talk with Holiday on June 7 and subsequently, while he was in Kentucky. And about seeing Holiday hand the gun to Banner immediately after the shooting.

"I didn't want them to be able to locate Holiday. I didn't want them to trace the gun. No gun, no crime."

And despite being offered a deal by ADA O'Keefe in 2007, Alejandro testifies, he refused at that time to appear in court.

"It wasn't even a thought at that time," he explains. "We were still friends. I was an active gang member. I took an oath."

Besides, testifying meant his family members still living in East River could be harmed.

"It changes their lives, not just mine."

When Holiday came back from Kentucky, Alejandro continued to hang out with him—never mentioning that he'd talked to the police. After his own release from prison in 2010 Alejandro was again in touch with Holiday. Then came the years of addiction to crack cocaine when "everyone disowned me"; his 2014 arrest; the fact that he was facing a sentence that could be as long as 12 years; and finally, the offer in 2015 to cooperate and tell the truth in court about the events of June 7, 2007.

Alejandro's entire personal history, the bullying and persecution he endured as a child, the periods of mental and emotional distress, the arrests and jail terms, the running away from treatment programs, the addiction to crack cocaine, the heavy usage of alcohol and PCP—all of this is fertile ground for Dawn Florio. In her cross examination she goes over and over his omissions and lies to police and to a grand jury. Isn't it the case that one motive in pointing the finger at Cucuta is to deflect investigation of his own possible role in the shooting? Isn't it true that smoking PCP so distorts perception that the smoker can see things that aren't there? That he can witness "events" that never happened? Hasn't he already violated the terms of his cooperation agreement by procuring and smoking marijuana?

But none of Florio's questions, accusations and insinuations can weaken the central point of Alejandro's testimony: Abraham Cucuta AKA Holiday, his friend and protector, a man with whom he spent hours and hours every single day—including the night of the murder—a man he described as meaning "everything to me," had shot Manuel Sabater while aiming at Booga, and had then executed Joshua Agard at point blank range. And he had personally witnessed these acts at a distance of ten feet.

CHAPTER 6

SUMMING UP: THE LAWYERS

Witnesses aside, a lot of the drama of a trial and perhaps much of its outcome rest on the shoulders of the opposing counsel. Attorney Dawn Florio, representing Abraham Cucuta, has a nearly impossible job. She'll be 55 a few days after trial ends, a practicing lawyer for 30 years—13 of those with the Bronx DA's office before switching to criminal defense.

In her cross-examination of Gabriel Washington and Alejandro Alvarez, Florio presses hard, confronting them with their sworn grand jury testimony, parts of which they were now, under oath, publicly repudiating. (On direct examination, both men acknowledged lying multiple times, to police and others.) She jousts with them about the effects of PCP (Alvarez readily admitted smoking PCP daily, while Washington denied ever smoking it), and gets the deputy medical examiner to confirm that this drug can alter reality and cause those smoking it to see things that aren't there.

But on the central, absolutely critical point, she fails to shake their identification of Cucuta as the perpetrator. Nor, in his defense, does she call a single witness who can testify that he was anywhere else but in the East River Houses courtyard when two young men were shot to death.

After the trial, when I finally connect with her after many calls and emails, she talks freely about her work as a defense lawyer and about her second, simultaneous career: selling beauty products and health supplements (which she herself uses) for a multilevel marketing company called Market America.

She got into this business four years ago, she tells me, as a result of her friendship with "Fat Joe," a rapper named Joseph Cartagena who's a celebrity spokesman at Market America conventions. Fat Joe had urged Florio to develop a second income because of her bad knees and the ordeal of being on her feet for hours each day of a trial. (Shortly after we talked, she underwent a hip replacement.)

Her Instagram and Facebook posts are full of accounts of her sales activities. In a post entitled "A Day in the Life: Dawn Florio" she writes about nightly parties and events at which she introduces Market America products to potential customers.

"I will not let a guest leave" until a follow up appointment is booked," she says.

At the time of our talk, Florio is nearing the end of another murder trial, her fourth or fifth since the Cucuta case; she's representing a rapper named Delona Jamison. (Accused of shooting three people after a club performance, Jamison is convicted of first-degree manslaughter two days later).

When she is on trial, "I don't do anything else but the trial, this is my life," she says.

A friend and fellow attorney, Fred Lichtmacher, calls Florio "as good a defense attorney as there is in New York." He tells me, "She is tireless, she works a tremendous number of hours per day, she's as well prepared as an attorney can be."

In The People vs. Cucuta, however, some of Florio's defense has a frenzied last-minute feel to it. The day before presenting her case, she spots two men from the neighborhood in court and hurriedly subpoenas them to testify. The idea, apparently, is to bolster the defense's insinuation that someone else, perhaps a mysterious man nicknamed Showtime, did the shooting. One of these witnesses is Shyce (Michael Kearse), the head of Sex Money Murder, but his testimony is absurd, so patently false that the jurors agree it does her case more harm than good

In contrast to Florio's passionate but light-on-facts defense, the prosecution's case is in the hands of a prosecutor who is meticulously organized. For me, and for most of my fellow jurors, the star of the trial is Assistant District Attorney Dafna Yoran.

Yoran began her career in the Manhattan DA's office in 1993 at the age of 28. Now, 25 years later, she's a senior trial lawyer with a special expertise in and passion for homicide cases. In September 2017 the New York County Lawyers Association gave her its Public Service Award, honoring lawyers in the public sector who are "role models, innovators and problem solvers."

Between 2011 and 2017, she prosecuted nine murder cases, all resulting in guilty verdicts. Defendants convicted under Yoran's hands-on trial management included Eugene Miller, guilty of the 2015 fatal shooting of ex-girlfriend Rosetta Ewell; Jeffrey Wong, sentenced to 25 years to life for the 2014 fatal stabbing of Khemraj Singh; and Bismark

Lithgow, convicted of second degree murder in the 2013 stabbing of his 19-year-old girlfriend, Francis Pellerano.

Yoran came to the U.S. from Israel with her parents and older sister at age 15. Within two years she had her undergraduate degree at NYU, then went on to a Master's in International Affairs from Columbia and a law degree from Brooklyn Law School.

Her mother and father escaped persecution and death at the hands of the Soviets and Nazis, respectively. In the 1920s, her mother Varda's family fled Russia for Tientsin, China. Yoran's father, born Selim Sznycer in Poland (in Israel he changed his name to Shalom Yoran), survived World War II hiding in the woods and joining partisan groups to fight the Germans. By mid-1944 he and his comrades were blowing up German troop trains, sometimes killing dozens or hundreds. His memoir, *The Defiant: A True Story of Jewish Vengeance & Survival* was published by St. Martin's Press in 1996. After the war he made his way to Palestine, later Israel, where he met and married Varda and where Dafna and her older sister Yaelle were born.

Watching her day after day from my front row seat in the jury box, I doubt Yoran would enjoy the same success at the poker table as in court. Her expressions during trial—ranging from intense concentration to amusement, irritation and utter disdain—are a dead giveaway to what she's thinking. In a game of seven-card stud with a pair of aces face up, her open-faced grin could be a clear signal that one of her hole cards is a third ace.

You can catch that grin in a February 2016 photo on her Facebook page. She's on vacation, floating in the turquoise waters off the impossibly white-sand beach of Vieques, an island eight miles from Puerto Rico. Supported by a blue noodle around her waist, wearing large sunglasses, a purple shirt and straw hat, Yoran sports an expression of giddy, almost child-like glee.

Yoran is short, about five-five, with a husky, I'm going to stand my ground voice. Thick strands of curly auburn hair hang loosely around the shoulders of her frumpy business suits; she seems too focused on matters at hand to bother taming those locks into a bun or a ponytail.

In the first days of The People vs. Abraham Cucuta trial she is neither dramatic nor especially eloquent, but she is all business. It's not until the end of the trial that Yoran's clarity of thought, persistence and powers of organization become clear. Her masterful summation disposes decisively of each of the defense's arguments, especially that the inconsistencies in some of the eye-witnesses' testimony render that testimony invalid. Yes, they had different recollections of what the shooter wore that night, ten and a half years ago, she acknowledges and then says to us in the jury box, You see me in court every day, right? Can you remember what I wore a few days ago? And if Abraham Cucuta had in fact covered part of his face with a bandana, as Gabriel Washington remembered, would that mean the witness couldn't reliably identify him? Holding a piece of fabric across her nose and mouth, she offers us jurors this clincher: "You still know it's me, don't you?"

She makes no attempt to deny what's missing (notably, the lack of physical evidence linking the defendant to the murder scene) but this omission is overwhelmed by the weight of the facts that are fitted to each other like hand-hewn stones, until they form a nearly impenetrable wall. To wit: the testimony of the two eyewitnesses (admittedly carefully coached), the accounts of detectives who interviewed those witnesses ten years earlier (when they admitted witnessing the killings but refused to testify), records documenting the hour and minute of the first 911 calls after the shootings. And the logs and maps of cellphone calls and direct-connects made by Cucuta in the hours and minutes before and after the shooting—maps that leave no doubt about his whereabouts on June 6 and 7, 2007.

The DA's office refuses my multiple requests to interview Yoran. But the person who has known her the longest, Varda Yoran, her 88-year-old mother, is happy to talk to me. Now widowed (her husband Shalom died in 2012) and living in a Frank Gehry-designed apartment building overlooking Brooklyn's Grand Army Plaza, Varda tells me that Dafna's fascination with public life and her concern for justice were apparent early. In Israel at age four, she asked her mother how she would go about preparing to "be Golda," i.e., to follow in the footsteps of Golda Meir, Israel's only woman prime minister.

As a child, Dafna and her sister were often present when their father's comrades, those who'd survived from the days of fighting the Germans, gathered to celebrate and reminisce. One oft-told story—whether true or apocryphal is impossible to know—was that of a woman about to be machine-gunned to death by the S.S. In that instant before she was tossed into a trench with thousands of other murdered Jews, the woman summoned the strength to scream at her Nazi executioners: "You will be held accountable."

All her childhood, Varda continues, Dafna was looking for, waiting for this accountability for the terrible crimes of the Nazis,

"And guess what? This is her profession, this is what she does. She holds murderers accountable for what they have done."

CHAPTER 7

OUR TURN

Trials drag. Three and a half weeks, even with Thursdays and Fridays off, is a long time to sit confined in our assigned seats in the jury box, as if obliged to watch a company of actors stage one scene after another until finally they figure out how to end the play. It's also many mornings in the jurors' room, chairs crowded around the long table, waiting for a straggler to show up, and when she does, waiting for the judge to call us in.

I'm tired of listening to words, tired of straining to hear witnesses. As for the lawyers who did most of the talking in this trial, they must be tired, too, not to mention a little hoarse. Judge Obus seems to be blessed with nearly limitless patience; still, I have to believe that he, too, wants to be done with this trial.

By the morning of December 19 closing statements are finished. Dawn Florio's is emotional, her voice rising with her fervor to discredit the prosecution case. Dafna Yoran's on the other hand, is closely reasoned. She gives us highlights from the eyewitness statements. She itemizes various items of evidence that support that testimony (notably the cellphone records). And she refutes one by one the defense's attempts to cast doubts on the witnesses' identification of Abraham Cucuta as the lone shooter.

In his charge to the jury, the judge explains the crux of our job: after all the evidence has been heard, and even if the preponderance of that evidence suggests that the defendant is guilty, if we still have a reasonable doubt we must acquit the defendant. In a criminal case preponderance of evidence is not sufficient.

He spends time defining the various possible verdicts. We must first decide whether the defendant is guilty of murder in the first degree for each of the victims. Only if we judge him not guilty on this count, for either victim, can we consider the charge of murder in the second degree. And only if we judge him not guilty of either first or second degree murder for either victim can we consider a charge of manslaughter.

The definition of murder in the first degree is simple to state, but it causes the jurors quite a bit of confusion in the jury room. The applicable language for the case before us holds that: A person is guilty of murder in the first degree when "With intent to cause the death of another person, he causes the death of such person or of a third person" and "in the same criminal transaction with intent to cause serious physical injury to or the death of an additional person or persons, causes the death of an additional person or persons." (Under the statute, there are a number of instances where no second death is required, e.g., if the victim was performing his or her official duties as a police officer, a judge, a firefighter, or was a witness to a crime and was killed to prevent his or her testimony or as retribution for that testimony.)

The lawyers have had their say, the judge has spoken; the defendant, as always, is silent. Now it's our turn. We file out of the jury box, accompanied by one of the uniformed officers. We take our seats around the table in the jurors' room. This time there are only 12 of us. The alternates are led into a separate room and will not be part of the deliberation.

In the past couple of days I've heard an occasional word or phrase from other jurors, wondering how long a deliberation we are in for, and whether there are indeed any of us who harbor a reasonable doubt about guilt. I have no doubt that Abraham Cucuta shot and killed two men on June 7, 2007. What I don't know is whether all jurors share my conviction.

Throughout the many hours we've spent in this room, our foreperson, Olivia, has kept to herself, rarely engaging in conversation with anyone else. And at this moment she has nothing to say, leaving it to others to speak up.

One of the leaders is Marc; at the time of the trial he's 45, with close-cropped reddish hair and a lean, focused look. It's an accident that he's on the jury.

"Ten times out of ten I'll do whatever it takes" to get excused from jury duty, he tells me afterward. His career has been in the financial service industry; he used to trade mortgage-backed securities, some of them secured by so-called liar loans; these were among the very instruments that caused the Great Recession of 2008. But as the jury was being selected he was between jobs.

"Since I had the time, I didn't mind doing it," he says.

Barely have we taken our seats before Marc suggests, quite forcefully, an immediate straw vote, by secret ballot, to see where we stand.

When no one balks at this, we pass out two small rectangles of paper. The vote is solely on the question: Is the defendant guilty or not of murder in the first degree, for each of the two victims? Each of us writes the name of each victim, Manuel Sabater, Joshua Agard, on a different piece of paper and then yes for guilty, no for not guilty. We fold the papers in half and pass them to the head of the table.

Finally the green board with the broken pieces of chalk has its moment: two names on the board, Joshua and Manuel, two headings under each name, guilty, not guilty, and Sophia, who teaches at PS 89 in Queens, standing in front of the class, recording our votes. The vertical chalk marks accumulate quickly. In the death of Joshua Agard there are 11 votes for guilty, one for not guilty. In the death of Manuel Sabater, however, the tally is seven yes, five no.

Silence for a few long seconds. Even for those of us convinced that Cucuta is guilty, it's a shock to see how much we agree. I suggest that we concentrate for now on Joshua Agard to see if we can identify the issue that is preventing a unanimous vote. Now Joselina speaks up; in the death of Joshua Agard hers was the lone not guilty vote. I'm just not sure he did it, she says, but why don't we go around the room so that I can hear the reasons of those who vote guilty.

Everyone has a say. We argue that the two eyewitnesses, Gabriel and Alejandro, had no incentive to lie; Gabriel actually signed his cooperation agreement several years before Cucuta's arrest and while that agreement makes him eligible for a somewhat reduced sentence, he still faces 18 more years in jail. We point out that their identification of the shooter hardly represents a recent aha moment. Ten years ago, in the weeks after the shooting, they actually told the police what they'd seen—while steadfastly refusing to testify at the time because of gang or personal loyalty, and fear of what happens to snitches. What's more, because both of them knew Cucuta so well, there can be no possibility of mistaken identity here. In fact, as they so often did, Cucuta and Alejandro were together for most of the afternoon and evening hours before the shooting, first working (assembling bags of drugs to sell on the street) and then relaxing (drinking, smoking marijuana and PCP).

And we bring up the cellphone records. Kristen, one of the younger jurors, is clear-headed and persuasive, not only about the credibility of the two eyewitnesses but about the map, a key prosecution exhibit, that shows where Cucuta's cellphone calls originated in the moments just before and just after the shooting.

Joselina appears swayed by our arguments, and reassured by the near-unanimity of opinion.

When we move on to discuss the death of Manuel Sabater, it's evident there is confusion about whether his killing falls under the definition of first-degree murder. His death was an accident; Cucuta was not aiming at him but rather at Wyatt Rudolph (Booga), the leader of the local Crips crew in Wilson Houses. How can an accidental death constitute murder in the first degree?

To resolve this question, we pass a note to the court officer asking Judge Obus to explain, again, the definition of murder in the first degree. For the next to last time we file into the courtroom. We take our assigned seats and again the judge reads the definition. He avoids interpretation or commentary. He doesn't say, So, even though the victim who died was not the target, if you find that the defendant intended to cause "serious physical injury to or the death of" an additional person and did in fact cause such a death, yes, that would constitute murder in the first degree. At the time I wonder why he isn't being more helpful; later I realize phrasing the issue in this way could be interpreted as nudging the jurors toward a particular verdict. Michael Obus is too intelligent and too experienced to allow his jury instructions to be grounds for an appeal.

Hearing the definition has the desired effect. The words "an additional person" need not refer to the intended target but to any person killed by the defendant's willful action. Those who voted not guilty in the death of Manuel Sabater agree that yes, this was murder in the first degree.

But now, even though we seem to have reached unanimous verdicts, there are still doubts. Sam, who agrees that Manuel's death fits the definition, has a question about the words, "as part of the same criminal transaction." The two shootings took place some minutes apart. Is this really "the same criminal transaction?" Once Sabater was shot accidentally, wasn't the deliberate execution of Joshua Agard a different transaction?

No single person hurls a bolt of clarity at this point but several of us respond.

Look, we say, testimony and cell records show that Cucuta left the East River Houses courtyard for a relatively short time around 4:30 A.M.; when he returned he had a gun and started firing at Booga. He intended to kill him; he wound up killing someone else—Manuel—and then, minutes later, he went on to kill a second person—Joshua—at point-blank range. It's not as if days or hours elapsed between these two deaths; both of them resulted from the same impulse, with the same weapon, in the same 10 or 15-minute period. Obviously these killings were, as the definition puts it, "part of the same criminal transaction."

Sam nods, gestures with his hands, speaks in his usual loud voice: Okay, I get it, I see.

But because once again we've referred to the cell-phone records and the all-important map, there's a desire on the part of Joselina, and one or two others, to look at those exhibits, to be sure, to be sure without a reasonable doubt.

Just when I think we were moving toward the finish line, now we halt. The finish line recedes. If the records are available, it can't do any harm to pause and look at them, can it?

And we pass another note to the officer, who brings it to the judge, and while this is happening we sit and wait.

The printouts of the cell records are voluminous; we barely glance at them. All eyes are on the prosecution's color-coded map and chart. They track Cucuta's calls minute by minute, from various locations in the courtyard before and after the shooting, and then, in the succeeding hours, all around the city: to the Upper West Side, to Chinatown, to Port Authority bus terminal, the trajectory of a man in a hurry to flee; he's looking for a bus that will take him west, to Kentucky and his girlfriend Betzy.

We can hear the echo of ADA Yoran's description of Abraham Cucuta's movements and her telling observation that from 9:15 A.M. on June 6 until 6:18 P.M. on June 7, hour after hour, almost minute by minute, he is constantly on his phone. Under extreme pressure, desperate to get away, for a period of 33 hours "he doesn't go to sleep!"

It's time. I'm pushing for a second vote, a public vote, on the question of guilty or not of murder in the first degree, in the death of Joshua Agard, in the death of Manuel Sabater. One by one we raise our hands: guilty on both counts.

As we file into the courtroom for the last time, I'm more nervous than I've been in the entire trial. I know the others feel the same way. The judge addresses Olivia as Madam Foreperson and when he asks for the verdict on the charge of murder in the first degree for each of the two victims, her voice is clear, not loud but not hesitant.

Dawn Florio seems momentarily stunned by what she has heard; she asks that the jury be polled. And one by one we pronounce the verdict on two counts of murder in the first degree: the word guilty, 24 times. When it's my turn I look at the defendant and speak louder than I should, a piece of theater that I regret—not the words but the insistence with which I pronounce them. We're delivering a verdict on the rest of a man's life and a little humility would have been more appropriate.

Back in the jury room we collect our coats and hats, scarves, backpacks; we're told to destroy our notes. The judge ducks into the room to thank us, and to tell us we are released from our vow of silence, we may talk about the case to anyone, including, if we want, the two parties or the press. And now, to give us some privacy, the court officer is taking us to a different elevator, one that will let us out through a side door a dozen paces from Centre Street rather than through the main entrance.

On this day, two days before the winter solstice, the afternoon light is beginning to wane; a late December sky will soon be turning dark. We now-former jurors scatter in different directions, some of us saying goodbye or shaking hands. It's a little like the leave-taking after a funeral when you realize that you have a life to live and had best make something of it.

But what I'm feeling is not the satisfaction of a job well done, not even a sense of completion but an emptiness tinged with despondence at the lives cut short or destined to be circumscribed by prison walls—the lives of the victims, the lives of the eyewitnesses and now the life of a convicted murderer—and I know that once again, as I've done every day after court but especially today, I have to clear my head by walking home.

CHAPTER 8

SPEAKING TO A CONVICTED MURDERER

Vanessa Cruz is a 32-year-old woman with a Master's in Special Education and a career in teaching young children with problems. She comes to court every day of the trial wearing jeans and stylish leather boots. She has perfectly coiffed black hair and clear skin the tone of light coffee. She takes her seat in the second row of the visitors' section, along with her grandmother, Maria Torres, and her aunt by marriage, Lisa Torres, who is in a wheelchair.

Maria Torres is the mother of the late Manuel Sabater, and Vanessa Cruz, her granddaughter, is Sabater's niece. Vanessa's own father, Jose Cruz, was the oldest of Maria's five children; Manuel was the youngest. Jose Cruz worked as a private guard on a security van that would make the rounds of stores, picking up the day's cash receipts for deposit. In 1994, at age 28, he was shot to death in the Bronx during an attempted robbery.

Though Vanessa lived with her mother on the Lower East Side, as a young girl she spent many weekends with her grandmother in Wilson Houses, across the street from East River Houses, and often saw her uncle Manuel, whose nickname in the family was Papito, or little papa. By the time Manuel was in his early teens, Vanessa recalls, he wasn't around the house much. He was busy selling drugs and, as time went on, in and out of jail.

When Abraham Cucuta was arrested in 2016, Dafna Yoran informed Maria Torres that her son's killer had been apprehended. On the first day of the trial, Maria and Vanessa meet the prosecutor for the first time as they sit on a bench in the wide corridor outside courtroom 1324. And every day thereafter, Yoran greets them warmly in advance of the court session and tells them what to expect from the day's testimony.

After the trial is over, I get a chance to sit down with Vanessa and Maria in a little coffee shop five blocks from the courtyard of East River Houses. As rain rattles the window looking out on Second Avenue, making me strain to hear her soft-spoken words, Maria shows me certificates and commendations that Manuel Sabater earned as an elementary school pupil at PS146. At that age he loved to draw. He was good in science. But by his early teens he was hanging out with men six, eight, ten years older, men who were selling drugs and who had a lot of money in their pockets. His mother tried but was powerless to steer him away from a lifestyle that she knew would bring trouble. What kind of trouble? Perhaps time in jail; as we talk she recalls warning him that if he were with men doing bad things, even if he didn't participate in them, he too would be arrested. Manuel was never a violent person, she tells me. The thought that trouble could mean a fatal bullet during a dice game at 4:30 in the morning never entered her mind.

Until she arrives for the trial, Vanessa has never laid eyes on Abraham Cucuta. Did she assume he was guilty because the prosecution had brought him to trial? She says no.

"I did go in with an open mind. When he came into the courtroom I looked at him. I had never seen him before. I didn't automatically assume he did it."

Ultimately, the testimony of the two eyewitnesses, and the cellphone records showing where Cucuta and others were making or receiving calls, convinced her of his guilt.

Vanessa Cruz attended PS 110 and JHS 56, then enrolled in St. Jean Baptiste on West 75th St., a Catholic girls' high school known for its college preparatory curriculum. She was always a good student, she says, "honor roll and everything." She got her Bachelor's from SUNY-New Paltz in 2008, a Master's in education from Hunter in 2014.

When the family of Manuel Sabater is given the opportunity to address the court prior to the Cucuta sentencing on February 22, it is Vanessa, niece of the murdered Manuel Sabater, daughter of a father who lost his life to violent crime, who rises to speak.

In her 15-minute remarks she addresses Cucuta directly.

"I have watched my grandmother grieve deeply over the loss of her youngest son and relive the nightmare of losing another child to gun violence. I have witnessed the pain in his son's eyes as he was faced with the reality of never seeing his father again. . . I know this pain all too well because I have experienced it as a child when my father was violently taken from me. Coincidentally our fathers were the same age when they were murdered, we were around the same age when it happened, and the men who committed their murders were under the influence of PCP. Let that sink in."

Despite her grandmother's deep anger over Manuel's senseless death, she continues, "she wants you to know she does not hate you; she hates your actions. She hopes that after this experience you will go on to change your life and make better choices" while in prison.

She urges Cucuta to take advantage of any opportunity "to mentor at-risk teens who are on the verge of making the same mistakes you have . . . [to] share your story with other inmates who still have the opportunity to be released from prison, so that they may make better choices and never return to prison" and to use your influence with current gang members "so another child like me or Manuel's son will not have to bury their parent."

Her plea has no effect. When Cucuta gets his chance to speak, he rants against everyone, accusing witnesses, police and assistant district attorneys of committing perjury during the trial. He shows no remorse for any action of his, neither in the present case, nor for the previous crimes for which he has been incarcerated. Against all evidence that I and 11 other jurors heard, he claims he had nothing to do with the murders.

Before he pronounces sentence, Judge Obus dwells briefly on Abraham Cucuta's behavior after the accidental shooting of Manuel Sabater: his deliberate, unprovoked and heartless execution of Joshua Agard, and now, his complete lack of remorse, and failure to accept the consequences of his actions. The evidence presented at trial was "more than sufficient" to justify the jury's decision, the judge notes, and he has no choice but to sentence Cucuta to life in prison without possibility of parole.

CHAPTER 9

THE SEARCH FOR WHY: NYCHA AND EAST RIVER HOUSES

Trials are about assessing guilt or innocence, not assigning blame. But at the end of The People vs. Abraham Cucuta, the question I'm left with is: Why? And there is plenty of blame to go around.

Above all there is the failure of families to do what families are supposed to do for their children. Gabriel and Alejandro were still children when they first began joining gangs, robbing tourists or peddling crack.

Then there is the failure of the public institutions whose job is to provide safe shelter free from vermin, mold and lead paint poisoning (and with reliable heat and hot water in winter); true educational opportunity for every child; protection from gangs, street violence and the criminal behavior of drug sellers.

These are, after all, the mandates of the New York City Housing Authority (NYCHA), the New York City Police Department (NYPD) and the New York City Department of Education (DOE). Can we assign these agencies at least some of the responsibility for the choices made by the victims, the witnesses and the defendant himself in the trial? Or do we give them a pass, and just put everything on men who father children and disappear to jail or to parts unknown, on women who smoke crack instead of taking vitamin pills and reading to their children?

East River Houses, the scene of the 2007 murders, is one of NYCHA's oldest projects. At one time or another, the defendant, the two key witnesses and one of the two victims, Manuel Sabater, lived either there or across the street in Wilson Houses. Do not visit the crime scene, Judge Obus has admonished the jurors again and again during the trial. And, despite my curiosity, during the three and a half weeks in court I heed his words.

But they no longer apply on this 11th day of January, a month after the end of the trial. It's a relatively mild afternoon, temperature in the mid-40s, a respite from three weeks of frigid winter weather. It's easy to recognize the housing project that was described in court testimony. Entering from East 102nd Street between First Avenue and the FDR Drive (this lower left quadrant is where PIRU sold its crack cocaine), I pick my way between patches of dirty snow, past the basketball court in the southern half of the courtyard, the children's playground in the northern half, and the concrete tables and benches where Abraham Cucuta sat eating and smoking PCP in the hours after midnight. Now I come to the low retaining wall, barely two feet high, in front of building 404. It was in the half-circle formed by this wall where five men rolled dice on the morning of June 7, 2007 and where two of them were killed in a barrage of bullets.

Ranged around the long courtyard are the ten dirty red-brick buildings that today house 2,416 residents in

1,170 apartments. Children 18 and under account for a little under a third of the total, or 766.

The sudden appearance of a swarm of boisterous teenagers at the far north end of the project near East 105th Street gives me an uneasy couple of seconds. Yet there are cops everywhere, assigned from PSA 5, the NYPD unit that patrols all NYCHA projects in East Harlem: two monitoring traffic at the intersection of First Avenue and East 102nd street, two posted on the corner of First Avenue and East 105th, and two more on the far side of the courtyard from 404, standing, watching.

As I wander East River Houses on occasional visits, there's no avoiding the signs of deterioration; dirty hallways, lights that need replacing, building numbers sometimes hidden behind boards tacked to a structure's exterior, a temporary fix for crumbling facades. I speak briefly with Joanne Figaro, the manager at East River. A 25-year veteran of NYCHA, she and her staff members (three housing assistants, two clerks) are busy with "the annuals," the paperwork tenants must resubmit every year documenting the income that qualifies them for rents as low as $250 per month. The offices, dingy and minimally furnished, are what I imagine the hangouts of the drug crews might look like, the bosses ready to flee the moment the cops come knocking.

"Of course after 70 years" East River Houses needs major maintenance, Figaro admits—but maintenance, she is quick to explain, is a different department and not under her direct control. Figaro also tells me that a tenant convicted of a crime is not allowed to live in a NYCHA project. But once again, she claims it's not her responsibility to enforce this.

"There's a process," she says.

If anything captures the "not my job" employee attitude that helps explain NYCHA's manifold failures, it is these words of the manager of East River Houses (she has since moved on to Lillian Wald Houses, a much larger NYCHA project on the Lower East Side where she is assistant manager). She manages...paperwork. The notion that she might bear some responsibility for, or take some action to bring about, badly needed repairs—or to prevent convicted criminals from plying their trade in the New York City housing development that is her responsibility—never seems to occur to her.

Some days later, in an interview in his apartment, Wilfred Thomas, president of the East River Tenants Association, insists to me that heat and hot water are not a problem in East River Houses; a new boiler provides plenty of both. Yet statistics supplied by NYCHA show that in the six months ending March 2018, the agency logged 824 "no heat" calls (seven calls for every 10 apartments), and 656 "no hot water" complaints at East River. In February 2018, city officials revealed that 320,000 residents in NYCHA projects citywide, or 80 percent of the total, had been without heat or hot water at some point during the current winter.

In January 2019, after previously admitting that "for years NYCHA has violated and continues to violate" federal health and safety regulations and "repeatedly made false statements to HUD and the public" about its failure of comply with lead paint rules, the City and NYCHA signed an agreement with the U.S. Attorney for the Southern District of New York. Under the supervision of a strong federal monitor, hired by HUD and paid by the City, the City agreed to spend $2.2 billion over ten years to repair NYCHA buildings and remediate five hazards detailed in the government's lawsuit—lead paint, mold, pest infestations, heating failures and inadequate elevators.

It was not always this way. East River Houses opened its doors in 1941, a spanking new development in a city desperate for clean, affordable housing, In 1941, more than 14,400 families applied for the first 1,170 apartments in East River Houses—13 times as many applicants as there were places. A photo from that year shows one of the happy winners, the Cerny family, gazing out the window of their new home. The husband is neatly attired in dark suit and tie, his wife in a polka dot dress and two young boys in knickers, short-sleeved shirts and heavy leather shoes, standard attire before sneakers became ubiquitous.

Novelist Richard Price grew up in the Parkside Houses in the Bronx. In an October 2014 article in *Guernica Magazine*, he recalls the 1950s and early 1960s as the golden age of public housing. A majority of tenants were working class, two-parent families; at the outset, only five to eight percent of NYCHA tenants were on welfare.

"Public housing," he points out, "had never been thought of as permanent housing. It was conceived as *springboard* housing . . . a working-class family would utilize their years in residence to raise children free of the mean streets and free enough from financial necessity to allow them to take their education all the way, after which they would have no need to ever return."

This vision began to fade in the 1960s as NYCHA accepted more and more welfare families, many of them headed by a single parent. The 1980s, Price, writes brought "the twin plagues of AIDS and crack, and an entire generation was lost to addiction, incarceration, and violent death." Instead of leaving, "generations began to stack up in the same apartment, each one faring economically worse than the last."

The picture of East River Houses and nearby Wilson, Washington and Jefferson Houses that emerges from the Cucuta trial is simply this: they were the headquarters of the drug crew bosses, their apartments provided the storerooms for the guns, and their courtyards and adjoining streets were the outdoor malls for the buying and selling of weed, crack, heroin and PCP.

It would be nice to think that after the events of June 2007, increased police presence in East River Houses and nearby projects, combined with the city-wide decline in crime, would have greatly reduced, if not eliminated, large-scale drug trafficking and related violence in East Harlem.

Nine years after the June 2007 murders, however, two huge takedowns involving the arrest of dozens of NYCHA residents showed that the projects continue to be a cauldron of crime.

On June 30, 2016, Manhattan DA Cyrus Vance and NYPD Commissioner Bill Bratton announced the arrest and indictment of 17 members of the 600/Gutta gang based in West Harlem, and 20 members of the East Army gang based in and around East River Houses, asserting that the gangs were engaged "in a bloody rivalry in Harlem and Upper Manhattan." Those arrested are alleged to be responsible for one homicide, 14 shootings and seven shooting victims

Just two months earlier, on April 19, Bratton and Preet Bharara, the U.S. Attorney for the Southern District, had heralded the arrest of 16 residents of East River Houses and 20 residents of Washington Houses. The indictments allege that the defendants trafficked in "heroin, crack cocaine, oxycodone and marijuana, peddled in all areas in and around the housing projects . . . and protected their lucrative businesses with guns and violence."

One of those arrested and charged in April was Abraham Cucuta AKA "Holiday." Here is the answer to what was Cucuta was doing in the months prior to the November 2017 trial: he was incarcerated in the Canaan federal prison in Waymart, PA, serving a sentence that runs until 2020. He had to be transported every day in the custody of officers, a trip taking several hours, before showing up at 100 Centre Street in neat slacks and checkered shirt, handcuffs removed. Only after he completes his term in federal prison will Cucuta be transferred to a state penitentiary where he will live out his days.

Despite the arrest of 36 East River Houses residents in the 2016 takedowns, the violence in and around East River persists—and, as in June 2007, the early morning hours are especially deadly.

At about 2 A.M. on February 15, 2018, less than a month after my first visit, 26-year-old Dwight Pitman was killed on East 105th Street, near his East River Houses apartment. Police say Pitman got into an argument with three men, one of whom shot him in the chest. NYPD officers tell me they know the killers but without eyewitnesses willing to testify, the DA's office will not authorize an arrest. And at 2:14 A.M. on September 4, 2018, Saveli Wilson, 26, was shot to death in front of building 404 at East River Houses; there have been no arrests in that killing either.

It's no mere coincidence that so many of these crimes—the double murder in June 2007, the two separate, fatal shootings 11 years later—take place between 2 A.M. and 4:30 A.M. Detective Billy Dunn of the 23rd precinct in East Harlem, who has seen it all, asks me, rhetorically, "Who do you think is out at four in the morning? Mother Theresa?"

Facing a tab to renovate its badly deteriorated housing stock—a tab that could run into tens of billions of dollars—NYCHA is now exploring a technique called RAD, for Rental Assistance Development, a way of handing over management of ailing projects to private developers who promise money for repairs, upgrading and new construction. In exchange, these developers gain the ability to build and convert some new units to middle-income market-rate housing, while preserving the rights of current tenants to their apartments at rental prices guaranteed not to exceed 30 percent of family income.

One such conversion at Ocean Bay (Bayside) Houses in Brooklyn has already taken place. Another, proposed for Fulton Houses in Manhattan—literally across the street from the hugely successful Chelsea Market—has provoked angry reactions from tenants there who fear being displaced and shunted aside. While the fears are understandable, this type of public-private partnership may be one way to tap the billions in private investment needed to rescue East River Houses, Washington Houses and other massive NYCHA projects in East Harlem.

CHAPTER 10

THE NYPD

Until the windup of my jury duty set me to exploring how young people in East Harlem wind up in trouble with the law, I'd only been in an NYPD precinct house once, and not with the desired results. Years ago, on the second floor of Precinct 6 on West 10th Street, Manhattan, a detective did his best to feign interest in my complaint: an unknown person had somehow accessed my bank account from an ATM in Queens, miles away, depleting the balance by hundreds of dollars. I had imagined swift, efficient police action—perhaps a camera had captured the image of the perpetrator, I suggested—but in fact, I never heard another word from the NYPD. (Yes, the bank replaced the stolen money.)

On my early 2018 visit to the community affairs unit at PSA 5, which patrols a dozen NYCHA housing projects in East Harlem, I'm seeking information, not crime-solving, and Detective Angel Lujan, officer Michael Vega and Lieutenant Adam Mellusi are happy to tell me about community policing. Lujan, Vega and their colleagues are talkative, appropriately cynical about the neighborhoods in which they work and seem to have all the time in the world to answer my earnest, if naive questions. Over the next 12 months I come back to PSA 5 twice for public forums, to find these same officers simultaneously welcoming and a bit incredulous that I still have questions about community policing. (On my last visit, Officer Vega informs me, with a self-conscious smile, that he's passed the sergeant's exam.)

Yes, they explain, there is police outreach to teens through the NYPD's Explore program, but most 13, 14 and 15-year-olds living in the projects are suspicious of or downright hostile to cops. Even those who'll accept an invitation to a Yankees or Knicks game (the NYPD gets free tickets) want to be dropped off, afterward, blocks from where they live. If friends see them hanging out with cops they might get branded as snitches, Mellusi points out.

Since 2015, the NYPD has named neighborhood coordination officers for each sector of a precinct like the 23rd, or an NYPD housing district like PSA 5. Local residents have the cellphone numbers of these NCOs and can call anytime they need help. Every precinct also holds a monthly community council meeting, open to anyone, and besides the meetings at PSA 5 I also attend a couple at Precinct 23. The residents who show up, mainly older people, get to question the precinct commander about anything on their minds. One incentive to attend: a free hot meal after all the talking is over. At PSA 5, most questions deal not with crime or police conduct, but with frustrations about the NYCHA projects—outdoor lights not being fixed, elevators out of service, piles of garbage that remain uncollected.

At first glance the precinct houses are humdrum places, seemingly not that different from tens of thousands of offices around the city—minus the wall to wall carpeting and better lighting of corporate America—where employees work at computers, sip coffee and share laughs. Except that those same employees, or at least their buddies in uniform, confront the rawness of the city daily, with unpredictable, sometimes lethal consequences.

The real work of the NYPD is outside, in the streets, in the buildings of East River, Washington and Jefferson Houses and in its response to late night calls about angry domestic quarrels, robberies, assaults—or shootings. The cops explain to me that when a report comes in of a loud disturbance at midnight in a NYCHA building, unless they are given an apartment number the responding officers have no choice but to "'do a vertical.'" They start at the top of a ten-story building and work their way down, knocking at doors on every floor. It's not a job that most of us would undertake, regardless of pay or benefits.

Every incident gets reported and tabulated, and it's from the analysis of those tabulations, particularly when the incident is criminal, that I begin to appreciate the immense contribution of modern-day data science (combined with top-down insistence on results) to enhancing public safety. The reduction in murders in New York City between 1990, when there were 2,605 homicides, and 2019, when there were 319, is a case study in statistics-based crime management and in holding commanders accountable.

Introduced in 1994 by then-commissioner Bill Bratton, CompStat charts every crime, precinct by precinct and block by block. CompStat is now highly digitized but in the early days it was paper-based. Black and white photographs of the CompStat meetings from the early 1990s show a conference room with stacks of reports, and a commander at the microphone being badgered about the crime numbers for his precinct. Now everything is online but the grillings are just as tough.

In the 23rd precinct, home to East River Houses, there were nine murders in 2000, ten in 2007, four in 2018 and two in 2019. Robberies, burglaries and auto thefts are down anywhere from 14 percent to 70 percent since 2007 but one category stands out for a disquieting rise. In the three precincts that make up East Harlem, the 23rd, the 25th and the 28th, felony assaults—crimes in which a victim suffers physical injury—have jumped 49 percent (63 percent in the 23d precinct alone) in those same 12 years. Clearly there are streets in East Harlem and hallways and courtyards in the NYCHA projects where it's best not to linger. At first I'm acutely aware of this fact, but after months of visits to East Harlem, I ignore it.

At a January 2019 breakfast meeting with the Police Foundation, Commissioner James O'Neill singled out East Harlem's 25th precinct as one of six where crime rates are twice as high as the city average. And he promised not to rest until "every block in every neighborhood enjoys the same level of safety and well-being as the rest of the city." Brownsville—he might have said East Harlem—"can and should be as safe as Brooklyn Heights."

One of the biggest obstacles to safe streets remains the unwillingness of witnesses to tell the police about a crime—and then to agree to testify in court. Detective Joshua Berish, who interviewed Alejandro Alvarez in the weeks after the June 7, 2007 killings, encounters this obstacle every day. As we talk in the 23rd precinct house,

Berish explains the nub of the problem. Again and again potential witnesses exhort him to "do your job," Berish tells me, while these same residents refuse to share what they know about a crime.

In the Cucuta case, while eventually admitting to Berish in 2007 that his buddy and protector had done the killing, Alavarez told one version after another, omitted vital details and of course, refused to testify until almost a decade had passed.

None of this is to deny that there are reasons why neighbors or associates won't talk. In New York as elsewhere, police corruption, misconduct and excessive force still occur, some cops lie on the witness stand, and there have been horrible instances of police shootings that kill otherwise harmless people.

And most importantly, witnesses rightly fear retribution, even death, at the hands of gang members if they go public.

Nevertheless, between the NYPD's community outreach efforts, its transparency about crime statistics—the latest CompStat numbers are posted online every week—and my conversations with officers, detectives and with Deputy Inspector Amir Yakatally, commander of PSA 5, I come away impressed by the responsiveness of the NYPD. Its officers have more contact, positive and negative, with neighborhood residents than almost any other city agency. And without a doubt the NYPD has made New York a lot safer.

The challenge of reducing crime in the NYCHA projects and surrounding neighborhoods of East Harlem remains formidable, however, and Dermot Shea, the new commissioner, may have second thoughts about repeating his predecessor's promise not to rest until Brownsville and East Harlem are as safe as Tribeca and Brooklyn Heights.

CHAPTER 11

THE EAST HARLEM SCHOOLS

Gabriel Washington and Alejandro Alvarez, the key witnesses in the Cucuta trial, both attended PS 146 on 106th Street between First Avenue and the FDR Drive, as did Manuel Sabater, one of the victims; it's the closest elementary school to East River and Wilson Houses and the obvious choice for parents. For all three young men, however, the streets, the gangs and the seemingly easy money from selling drugs provided lessons more compelling, if ultimately much more tragic, than what they learned in the classroom.

In the aftermath of the trial, I ask myself: Would a better education have given these young men a path out of truancy, juvenile crime and incarceration? It's an ingenuous question, deliberately so, because it ignores all the other influences in their lives: the violence that prompts some to join gangs for self-protection, the fat rolls of twenties and fifties in their pockets from peddling crack, the often inadequate or absent parental supervision. But it's not an absurd question. Not when the laws say every child must stay in school until at least age 16. Not when, in New York City, we spend upwards of $25,000 per child per year on that schooling. (New York State, in fact, spends twice as much per pupil as the national average and more than any other state.)

In the weeks and months after the trial, this question about the role of the schools nags at me until it becomes an obsession. I visit or talk to teachers, principals or parents of students at seven DOE and two charter schools in District 4, East Harlem, and four high-performing high schools (two DOE, one charter, one Catholic) elsewhere in the city. I pore over enrollment, attendance and standardized test results for every school in District 4 until I am drowning in data.

And while the numbers help me to grasp the magnitude of the problem, it's only by seeking out successful schools in East Harlem that I fumble my way toward understanding how in fact it's possible to help children who deserve better. Better than the experience of Gabriel Washington who by age 12 was cutting school with impunity, sliding easily into petty crime, and ultimately, felony murder. Better than that of Alejandro Alvarez, who was bullied mercilessly by classmates, and who, while still in elementary school, took to the streets to steal and to sleep in subway cars.

Meanwhile, the picture of District 4 is coming into focus. With nearly 13,000 children enrolled in DOE schools, it is not the worst-performing of the 32 regular school districts in the city; that sad label belongs to District 12. (Of the five with the lowest scores, Districts 7, 9 and 12 are in the Bronx; District 23 is in Brownsville, Brooklyn; and District 5, Central Harlem, is in Manhattan.)

On 2019 state tests, District 4 ranks 18th out of 32 districts in English Language Arts (ELA) and 19th in math. And although on paper 42 percent of District 4 students are proficient in ELA and 36.8 percent in math, those numbers don't tell the whole story. First, the state made the tests easier in 2016 and again, in 2019, so apparent gains from one year to the next may not be real. (While state tests seem to register improvement, the National Assessment of Educational Progress tests, administered annually to a sample of students across the nation and known as the gold standard, show no gains in New York City scores between 2009 and 2019—and a large, persistent gap between scores of white and Asian students, and scores of black and Latino children)

Second, out of 23 DOE schools in District 4, two top-performers, PS 12 and PS/IS 171, account for one-third or more of the proficient students, an astounding share. Proficiency rates for the remaining 21 are just 37.8 percent in ELA, and 28.1 percent in math. Indeed, at only four of the 23 schools are a majority of students proficient in math, and at only six are a majority proficient in ELA.

Third—and crucially—many children who would likely do very poorly on state tests never take them. In 2018–19, of 5,870 third through eighth graders in District 4, fewer than 4,800 actually sat for either the ELA or math tests. Absenteeism is a huge educational and social problem in District 4: 29 percent of students are chronically absent, vs. 9 percent in high-performing District 2 in Manhattan. At a few District 4 schools, chronic absenteeism approaches or exceeds 40 percent.

Meanwhile, enrollment in District 4 schools has been dropping as charter enrollment surges. The DOE head count is down by 1,230 children since 2013–14; in the same period, charters have added 2,300 students. They now enroll 33 percent of the DOE-charter total, up from 21 percent five years ago—a powerful illustration of parents voting with their feet to choose what they believe is best for their children.

With these numbers as a backdrop, it becomes more urgent than ever for me to understand not the failures but the successes. A few schools in East Harlem are doing an exceptional job—family and social problems notwithstanding. And I wonder, what's their secret?

My visit to PS/IS 171 Patrick Henry, an elementary and middle school at the corner of East 103d Street and Madison Avenue, is an eye-opener: 171 is a standout in East Harlem, with 74 percent of its students proficient in math, 73 percent proficient in ELA. No other regular DOE school comes close.

Dimitres Pantelidis, the tireless principal of PS 171 for the past 15 years, is known for an approach called data-driven instruction (DDI), involving teacher-developed curricula and constant goal-setting and evaluation, student by student. When vacancies occur (usually just a few each year), he takes great pains with teacher selection.

"I've learned," he says, "to be very, very careful about bringing on a new educator."

When Pantelidis invites me to visit his school, he urges me to be there by 7:30 A.M., which is when he stands outside every morning to greet each arriving student. His own workday begins several hours before sunup (he answers one of my emails at 4:07 A.M., another at 4:11 A.M.) and doesn't end until five or six in the evening.

He is intensely focused on each child: "Anything less than 100 percent is not enough. It only takes one human being to change a kid's life."

On a subsequent visit, late in the school year, I spend some time with Neris Roldan, a second-grade teacher with 20 years' teaching experience at PS 171, and with Rachel Cohn, a first-grade teacher finishing her first year at the school (though she has several years' experience teaching elsewhere). In each of their classes, students are reading about a nonfiction topic—but with different texts keyed to their various reading levels. Teachers at PS 171 work together to develop the appropriate curriculum for their classes, and a hallmark of that curriculum is that it can be individualized to meet the needs of each child.

Like many of the children at PS 171, and in East Harlem generally, Pantelidis is the child of immigrants; he arrived in the U.S. at the age of three. But unlike the families of his students, Pantelidis' parents did not come from Puerto Rico, the Dominican Republic, various Central and South American countries or Bangladesh. They came from Greece, from "a very small island called Leros," he explains, and settled in Astoria, Queens, which was then home to many Greek families. (Strolling up and down Broadway and Steinway Street these days, you are more likely to hear Spanish, Bengali, Arabic, Urdu or Russian than to encounter Greek speakers.)

Neither of his parents had more than an elementary school education. His father did janitorial work in the Sabrett bread plant in East Rutherford, NJ while his mother supervised orders and shipments at a small dress factory in Queens. Pantelidis attended PS 17, Junior High School 10 and William Cullen Bryant High School, all nearby in Queens, in the days when almost all students went to zoned schools.

"I had a passion for learning," he says, "and what really inspired me was the hard work that my parents put forth. When you get to see your parents working hard you want to really make them proud."

By senior year of high school he was taking advanced Regents' classes. He went to Hunter for his B.A. (1991), a Master's in Education (1994) and then for a degree in administration (1997). After eight years as a teacher and staff developer at PS 108 in East Harlem, in 1999 Pantelidis was tapped to be an assistant principal at Patrick Henry. Two years later he became principal.

His toughest challenge was establishing trust with teachers, many of them older, some wondering what they had to learn from a young man the same age as their sons.

The solution? "We had discussions, we went on visitations, we talked about instruction."

A key influence for Pantelidis was a professor at Hunter, Dr. George Gonzalez, with whom he had a special relationship. Says Pantelidis: "He would call me every single day at five o'clock in the morning to ask, 'What are you planning for today?'" Often on Fridays, Gonzalez would accompany Pantelidis and the assistant principals on classroom visits.

"He would always tell me, 'We have to come in with a specific focus.' This the way that I work now, with a lens: What are you looking at today, are you looking at questioning, are you looking at engagement, are you looking at closure?"

Even on the phone, the third or fourth time we've had such conversations, Pantelidis still conveys his enthusiasm for the nuts and bolts, the daily grind: greeting students at 7:30 A.M., working with his APs, teachers, his data team (how many elementary-middle school principals have a data team?) and never sounding or looking anything but serious and business-like. (On my second visit, he's wearing a dark suit with a tie and pocket square, both in lavender, that match it perfectly.)

Yes, he often beams with pride about the school; the office and the narrow hallways are festooned with blown-up newspaper clippings, plaques, city and state awards, all attesting to 171's outstanding performance. But he's not one for the sly joke or the ironic aside. It's easy for educators to be cynical about the endless bureaucratic rigmarole, but instead, Pantelidis conveys an upbeat earnestness that wins me over—and sets me lamenting that more principals in East Harlem can't come close to matching his results.

Besides his high expectations for classroom learning, Pantelidis has set up partnerships with a range of outside partners, e.g., Urban Advantage (field trips to the American Museum of Natural History and the New York Hall of Science), Chess in the Schools, Mount Sinai School of Medicine (where middle schoolers can experience what goes on in research labs), and the Carmel Hill Fund (scholarships for summer study at Vassar and Yale).

Pantelidis and his family live in Bayside, Queens. On nearly empty streets in the dark hours before 4 A.M. it takes him barely 20 minutes to make the drive to East 103d Street; at rush hour the trip home can take more than an hour. His son is a freshman at S. John's; his daughter Marina, with a Bachelor's and Master's from Adelphi, has just begun teaching English at IS 126 in Astoria.

"I didn't want her to be a teacher, so much is expected of teachers now," he confesses, "but she said, 'This is what I want to do,' and it gives me a really nice feeling."

Beyond PS 171, it's hard to find District 4 schools that consistently outperform. Teacher or principal turnover and enrollment shifts can quickly hurt results at a school that was doing well.

At PS 37 River East, at First Avenue near East 120th Street, which also accepts children from the Bronx and the Upper East Side, a majority of pupils were proficient in ELA (51 percent) and nearing proficiency in math (45 percent) in 2017 and 2018. In 2018–19 when the school moved to its current larger building, many more children from the immediate neighborhood enrolled and on 2019 tests, proficiency rates dropped sharply, to 36 percent in ELA, 21 percent in math. It was a jarring decline, principal Michael Panetta acknowledges to me, and prompted him to reengage with Teachers College for professional development, and to beef up reading instruction.

Two middle schools that screen for admission, tiny MS 610 Young Women's Leadership School (also a high school) and MS 224 Manhattan School East, boast above-average 2019 proficiency rates. Then there's PS 83 Luis Munoz Rivera, at 219 East 109th Street, which ranks sixth among District 4 schools in ELA proficiency (50 percent) and third in math (56 percent).

Unlike some other district schools where enrollment has fallen by a quarter, a third or even more since 2013, PS 83 is holding onto its students. Principal Frances Castillo commands the trust of teachers and parents by the intensity of her commitment to children and to the community, says Susan Kowal, a veteran first grade teacher. Castillo, she adds, "is the kind of woman who goes shopping [with her own money] at Christmas time to make sure that every kid" gets a gift.

Finally, while it's true that at several District 4 schools 50 percent or more of the students are at or near grade level, this is hardly cause for cheering. Even at these schools, hundreds of children will still lack basic reading and math skills by the time they finish eighth grade.

At PS 171, "anything less than 100 percent is not good enough," Dimitres Pantelidis insisted to me—just as it wouldn't be good enough in Brooklyn Heights or Douglaston, Queens. How many other principals share his impatience that even with 74 percent of children at grade level there's still work to do?

Among high schools, Central Park East High School on East 106th Street and Madison Avenue is a striking success. Graduation rates have risen from the low 30s when principal Bennett Lieberman took over in 2005 to 100 percent in 2019. In selecting students, 75 percent of whom are black or Latino, the school emphasizes attendance and grades, not standardized test scores. College prep is a focus from day one; peer mentoring pairs freshmen with older students; and this small school of just 500 students offers an astonishing range of clubs, sports and activities. Teacher turnover is almost nil.

There are numerous scholarships available to CPEHS students for summer study at various colleges, a full-time college counselor and her assistants strive to match seniors to just the right school and almost all students go on to two or four-year colleges, including Brown, Columbia and University of Chicago. One highlight: 97 percent of graduates from the CPEHS class of 2016 were still enrolled in college 18 months after entrance, a persistence rate that is rare among students from low-income families.

Lieberman, 52, a former Social Studies and English teacher, is reflective and low-key. He jokes, "I've actually been principal of three schools, a failing school from 2005 to 2008, a so-so school from 2009 to 2011 or 2012, and now a successful school." The word is out: in 2005 CPEHS got barely 200 applications for 125 to 130 freshman places. In 2018 it got 5,400.

Charter Schools in District 4

IN MY quest for success stories in District 4 I also visit two charter schools. At Dream Charter School (elementary and middle grades) on Second Avenue and 103rd Street, Eve Colavito, Chief Education Officer, consistently meets her goal of enrolling at least 50 percent of incoming students from the poorest environments, i.e., NYCHA projects, including East River Houses and Washington Houses. She's a proponent of social-emotional learning and of close relations with and support of families. With a big push on literacy in kindergarten and early elementary grades, Dream had been boosting student performance year by year through 2018, when proficiency rates in both math and ELA were 54 percent. Then, on the spring 2019 tests, the ELA rate dropped to 49 percent. Colavito brushes this off, saying results for grades 5, 6 and 7 were affected by the arrival of a new middle school principal, a new academic dean and teacher turnover due to maternity leaves.

Dream has the feel of an upscale suburban school, with its wide gleaming halls, its busy offices, the agreeable hum (rarely rising to the level of distraction) of pupils and teachers moving from class to class. I drop in on Alexandra Brown's third grade class where students are literally racing against a clock, the seconds flashing by in red, to solve a math problem. When they come to the board to show their answers, what's especially important is that they include their step by step method for arriving at it.

Brown, the daughter of educators, has taught for five years at Dream and exudes purposeful authority and commitment to her students. In front of her class she stands tall (five-eight and a half) with perfect posture; I can picture her mother reminding her at meals to sit up straight, no slouching,

In fall 2019, she moved to Dream's new charter school in the Mott Haven section of the Bronx where, for the first time, she is teaching kindergarten—and relishing the challenge of a new school and the excitement of helping children learn to read and write their own names.

A contentious issue in education these days is whether black and Latino children learn better if their teachers are women (or men) of color. I pose this question to Alexandra Brown, herself African-American, and the answer is nuanced: "I think it could be true" in some cases, but "overall the more important thing is just the relationship you are able to develop with your students, to see that yes, these people may dress a little bit differently and look a little bit different . . . but people that are able to recognize that and move on from that" can be successful, regardless of their skin color.

Her own background illustrates that this challenge is not just theoretical. Brown grew up in Pequannock, a small northern New Jersey town. Her neighbors and fellow students were mostly white. Her father taught history and coached basketball and track in Rye, NY, an upscale Westchester county suburb where median household income is $172,000. (In East Harlem, the comparable number is $37,000.) After graduating from the College of New Jersey, Brown spent two years in Teach for America: first training and student teaching and then, her own class, all at Dream Charter School; along the way she earned her Master's degree.

Teaching full-time at Dream inevitably occasioned a bit of culture shock, she recalls, heightened by the difference between her own middle class upbringing, where two parents were always present, and the home lives of her students.

"Little things like getting to school on time, that was really hard. I was never late to school, my parents drove me. It was weird" to see children showing up 30 or 40 minutes late. Through home visits to children in her class, Brown got to see "who the child is living with and who they are around most of the time." These visits ended up "shifting my view about what family is," helping her to understand behavior that at first seemed puzzling.

My other charter school visit is to Success Academy Harlem 3, located on East 100th Street between First Avenue and the FDR Drive and part of Eva Moskowitz's Success Academy network. Here I see an orderly, brightly lit school that aims unabashedly to help every child perform at the highest academic level. In the Success Academy playbook, parental commitment and involvement are key. Tara Stant, principal for the past five years, says all parents attend an introductory session, often hosted by Moskowitz herself, so they know what to expect.

At the time of my visit, I don't yet know that what is expected includes, among other things, the no-exceptions obligation to read six books a week aloud to their young children. Even for Stant, matter-of-fact rather than boastful, it is quite the understatement when she says, "It's not that you drop off your child and the school does the rest."

Success Academy's disciplined, highly structured environment—uniforms, the silent movement of pupils from one room to another, its insistence that 100 percent of the time children must "track," i.e., keep their eyes focused on the teacher—is not for everyone. But for families that embrace it, there is no denying the results. At Harlem 3 (grades K-4) and the companion Harlem East Middle School (5-8), 99 percent of students are proficient in math, 89 percent in ELA, numbers that no regular DOE or charter school in East Harlem (nor few anywhere in the city or state) can match. The one exception among the DOE schools in District 4 is the talented and gifted school, PS 12 Young Scholars, which admits by competitive exam and has proficiency rates in the high 90s.

At eight charters enrolling elementary and/or middle school pupils in District 4, median proficiency rates on 2019 tests were 43 percent in ELA and 47 percent in math—markedly better than the DOE medians, but again, no cause for celebration; the numbers were dragged down by results at two low-performing charters, Capital Preparatory and Harbor. Among charters, the huge gap in math proficiency between Harlem 3 (99 percent) and second-best Amber Charter School (58 percent) reinforces the takeaway: like many a world record holder, Success Academy is really competing only against itself.*

---

*For insights into how Success Academy does it, I'm indebted to Robert Pondiscio's excellent book, *How the Other Half Learns: Equality, Excellence and the Battle Over School Choice* (Penguin Random House, 2019)

High-performing schools like PS 171, PS 83, Success Academy Harlem 3 and Central Park East High School all have a student body that is at least 75 percent Latino and black, and mostly from low-income families, closely matching the makeup of East Harlem and the NYCHA projects.

But these schools are the exceptions. PS 146, the default for East River Houses children, has seen proficiency rates rise since 2017 (again, the later numbers are not truly comparable) but even in 2019, 63 percent of children are not proficient in math, while 69 percent fall short in ELA. Attendance at 146 is poor: 37 percent of students are chronically absent.

Like many East River Houses parents, Denikqua Berry sent her twin daughters to kindergarten at nearby PS 146. For first grade, Berry pulled them out. The teachers, she tells me, weren't really communicating with her about her children. "I wasn't happy," she says. "I thought it was not a good experience for them." By lottery they gained admission to Dream Charter School.

Another East Harlem parent who switched her child out of 146 is Lisa Torres; her nine-year-old son moved to PS 83 in September 2018. Torres tells me that at PS 146 he was "starting to follow the wrong kids, the kids who always get into trouble."

I try to interview Mona Silfen, principal of PS 146. None of my calls or emails are returned, neither by her nor by District Superintendent Alexandra Estrella. After multiple requests, the DOE press office gives me my answer: No.

Pathways to Educational Success

ONE OF the more intriguing data points on the DOE's School Quality Snapshot is the percentage of teachers who trust their principal. I looked at this number for the bottom eight District 4 schools, ranked by ELA proficiency in 2017–18. At those eight, the percentage of teachers trusting the principal in 2018 ranged from a high of 98 percent (PS 108) to a low of 58 percent (PS 375); the median was 78 percent. But what a difference at the top eight schools; here the percentage of teachers trusting the principal ranged from a high of 100 percent (Central Park East I) to a low of 71 percent (MS 224); the median was 92.5 percent. At only one of the top eight schools did fewer than 75 percent of teachers express trust in the principal. At the bottom eight, four schools fell below 75 percent. At PS 146, only 39 percent of teachers expressed trust in the principal in 2017. Although the percentage rose to 74 percent in 2018, fully a third of teachers at the school did not answer the question in the latter year.

Is it really a surprise that the quality of school leadership, the sense of *esprit de corps*, the degree of alignment between principal and teachers, and the absolute, unvarying commitment to reach every single child are the essential ingredients in school success?

In an interview, State Assemblyman Robert Rodriguez, who represents Assembly District 68, East Harlem, put particular emphasis on educational opportunity and choice. Rodriguez grew up in East Harlem, attended River East Elementary School, went on to Cardinal Hayes High School and to Yale for his BA and NYU for an MBA. Lamenting the closing of Catholic high schools like Mother Cabrini and St. Agnes, Rodriguez says, "I think it's important to have a variety of choices"—he mentions charters and Catholic schools—"not just your local elementary schools."

Is there enough choice for parents today? I ask.

"Until you find the school that fits your child perfectly, I would say no."

One promising initiative in New York is the preK program that now allows any four-year-old to attend preschool free of charge. Clearly there is benefit to offering socialization and early learning to all children, especially those in low-income areas. And with 68,000 children enrolled in full-day preK programs in 2018–19, and another 6,000 in half-day, New York (along with Washington, DC) stands out for reaching nearly 100 percent of the city's population of four-year-olds.

The DOE cites improvement in the program since 2013–14, but Jeanne L. Reid, a research scientist and early childhood expert at Teachers College, Columbia University, cautions that her own studies show considerable variation from one site to another, and especially between classes in DOE schools and those in community settings (given lack of space at various DOE schools, independent community-based organizations actually enroll 60 percent of the children in preK.). There is reason for hope—but on my part, considerable skepticism—about the long-term impact of preK and now, its extension to three-year-olds. The reason? Gains from these programs can readily evaporate if too many children wind up in failing K-5 elementary schools.

Of all the obstacles to improving educational outcomes for children in East Harlem, one gets little attention, perhaps because it is so pervasive that it goes unrecognized. This is the mentality of "good enough." When most children in District 4 lack basic proficiency in reading and math, it becomes easy to assume that getting to 50 percent is the goal. Thus, year after year, policymakers from the mayor and chancellor on down hail an improvement in the number of children reaching proficiency—even when that "improvement" is a couple of percentage points on a test that is easier than the test given a few years before.

Leaders of the two highest-performing schools in District 4 (not counting PS 12), Dimitres Pantelidis at PS 171 Patrick Henry and Tara Stant at Success Academy Harlem 3, openly proclaim that their goal is not 50 percent but 100 percent. They take pride that their schools rank not just above the median but among the best schools in New York State.

According to Joseph Johnson, who founded the National Center for Urban School Transformation at San Diego State University, and who is now University Provost, one goal of NCUST's America's Best Urban Schools award (given to PS 171 Patrick Henry, among others, in 2018) is to create "cognitive dissonance" among educational leaders.

Too often, he explains in an interview, leaders "don't believe that such success [i.e., 100 percent proficiency] is possible . . . I mean leaders at all levels, up and down the system." They look at the data from better-performing schools and say "this isn't bad" for this population of students. By showing that a high level of success is possible, Johnson argues, the example of a PS 171 can push educators to reevaluate assumptions about what children from poor families can achieve.

In the real world, unfortunately, such results often invite the criticism that behind apparent success lies some trick, some quirk of measurement, some controversial practice (like the Success Academy focus on discipline or test prep). In a perverse distortion of reality, instead of representing a benchmark to which other educators might aspire, the highly successful schools may even become a target of disparagement.

"If only," their critics complain, if only we had such motivated children from supportive families in our schools, if only (like some charter networks) we had billionaire supporters to pour money into special staff and services, naturally we could do as well. Yet if the lesson of these successful schools means anything, it's that there's nothing natural about extraordinary results.

Of course, scores on standardized tests should not be the sole, or even the most important, measure of a child's success. In his book, *How Children Succeed**, writer Paul Tough describes how David Levin, a co-founder of the KIPP (Knowledge is Power Program) charter network, wrestled with the mystery of character and its effect on children's success in school and in life.

Levin was fascinated by psychologist Martin Seligman's book, *Learned Optimism***, which argues that character traits (like optimism) are not inborn but can be learned. His quest for the "right" character traits grew out of his shock at how students of KIPP Academy, his very high-performing charter middle school in the South Bronx, fared in college. Almost all of the first graduates at KIPP Academy (Class of 1999) went on to finish high school and enter college. But six years after high school, only 21 percent had a college degree, a dismal performance.

*Paul Tough, *How Children Succeed* (Houghton Mifflin, 2012)
**Martin Seligman, *Learned Optimism* (Knopf, 1991; Vintage paperback, 2006)

Citing the work of Seligman and of a psychology professor named Angela Duckworth, Tough zeros in on two character traits that correlate well with success in life: conscientiousness, the ability to focus on the task at hand, and grit, the determination to persevere despite setbacks.

My own example of grit comes from Manhattan Village Academy. In spring 2019, news that only seven black students (out of 895 students admitted) had scored high enough on the daunting Special High Schools Admissions Test (SHSAT) to gain entry to Stuyvesant High School caused an uproar. The *New York Times,* the mayor and others demanded changes in the admissions criteria to Stuyvesant, Bronx Science and Brooklyn Tech. Perplexed by this simplistic view of the problem, I sought out high schools where black and Latino students excel. My article, "Look Beyond Stuyvesant," appeared in the *New York Daily News* on April 28, 2019.

"The real failure of the Department of Education," it said, was not the low admission rate of minority students to Stuyvesant but "the unacceptable performance of many elementary and middle schools" serving children in the South Bronx, Brownsville and other poor neighborhoods.

Besides Central Park East High School in District 4, another outstanding high school profiled in the article—also with a mostly Latino and black student body—is Manhattan Village Academy on West 22nd Street in Chelsea. MVA, which admits students from all over the city, receives thousands of applications for 100+ freshman spots. In evaluating applicants, the demanding principal, Hector Geager, pays little attention to test scores. To him the best predictor of success is perfect attendance. He tells me in a single word what he is looking for: "grit."

Leadership at the Top: A Tale of Three Chancellors

Such successes, real but scattered, make me ponder a key question for the future of children—not only in District 4 but elsewhere: How critical is the right leadership at the top of the largest urban school system? Because this too can affect a Gabriel Washington or an Alejandro Alvarez.

Specifically, what influence can the person at the top wield when he or she is responsible for 1 million children, 1,667 schools, 6,000-plus principals, 78,000 classroom teachers and 19,000 other paraprofessionals in the schools? Does this mammoth $34-billion enterprise (plus a separate $17 billion capital budget), spanning every neighborhood, ethnic group and income level, defy the ability of any one person to manage it? If the DOE were a public company, its $51 billion budget would put it in 63rd place by revenues in the Fortune 500, behind Goldman Sachs and ahead of Morgan Stanley. But no for-profit company faces the challenges of the school system: a unique social mission; its million-plus customers, with varied needs, capabilities and often, handicaps; parents who rightfully want a say in their children's education; a militant teachers' union and city and state politicians and state education officials, all with the power to affect how schools are run.

In 2002, when Michael Bloomberg became mayor, the state legislature passed and the governor signed a law authorizing mayoral control of the schools. As his chancellor of the renamed Department of Education, Bloomberg picked Joel Klein, former Assistant U.S. Attorney General in charge of the antitrust division at the U.S. Department of Justice. Klein, who had little experience in education, served eight years, longer than any of the

22 other people who have held the job (previously called superintendent) since 1960. When he left in 2010, the school system was a very different place.

Klein's tenure was marked by energetic, often confrontational efforts to upset the status quo, to champion new leadership styles and autonomy for principals and above all, to insist on the importance of data in evaluating individual schools and the system as a whole. Every school got a report card and a letter grade, making it easy for parents to compare schools but provoking intense criticism of the grades and their methodology.

He closed more than 150 poor-performing schools, among them 29 high schools, opened hundreds of new ones, many of them small, and, with Bloomberg, championed the growth of charter schools as an alternative for parents in poor neighborhoods. The number of charters soared from 18 enrolling 4,442 students in 2002 to 159 with 58,493 students ten years later.

The bolder the educational agenda of the mayor and chancellor, the more pushback they engender. One redoubtable Klein opponent was Randi Weingarten, president of the United Federation of Teachers. Another critic, writer and education historian Diane Ravitch, has denounced the charter school movement and other "reforms" as an attempt by billionaires "to disrupt, reinvent and redesign" public education. In her latest book, *Slaying Goliath** she applauds "parent and teacher resistance to the chaotic reign" of Bloomberg and Klein.

By contrast, in a 2015 review of Klein's book, *Lessons of Hope*, David Steiner, the former New York State

---

*Diane Ravtich, *Slaying Goliath* (Knopf, 2020)
**Joel Klein, *Lessons of Hope* (Harper, 2014) reviewed by David Steiner in *Education Next*, Summer 2015

education commissioner, wrote: "I believe there is simply no doubt that under Klein's leadership, children attending public schools in New York City were, on average, being far better educated at the end of his eight years than they had been nine years before."

When I ask whether he still agrees with that assessment, he answers concisely, "I still agree."

Mayor Bill de Blasio set out to reverse many of the Bloomberg-Klein policies, including letter grades for schools and the wholesale closing of low-performing schools. He sought to change the admissions criteria for the city's selective high schools in order to admit more black and Latino students. He championed preK and opposed the growth of charter schools. His ambitious plan to revitalize 94 failing schools across the city, dubbed the Renewal School program, cost $773 million over four years but had little effect on student performance.

De Blasio's first chancellor, Carmen Fariña, had 40 years' experience as a teacher, principal and deputy chancellor. During her three-year tenure she visited schools all over the city and once told DOE staff members who were analyzing spreadsheets to identify successful schools, "I know a good school when I'm in the building." Her low-key approach introduced a period of relative calm between two highly controversial chancellors.

De Blasio's March 2018 appointment of Richard Carranza as the next chancellor signaled a stark change in tone and mission. In an early interview with *Chalkbeat*, the education newsletter, Carranza insisted that segregation, whether by race or by academic level, that has the effect of clustering mostly white and Asian students in a small number of high schools "is not acceptable." It was a declaration that he would repeat insistently and defiantly.

Within a month of Carranza's appointment the DOE announced it would spend $23 million on anti-bias training for its employees. One of the consultants who conducted this training, Glenn Singleton, wrote in his book, *Courageous Conversations*, that "the most devastating factor contributing to the lowered achievement of students of color is institutionalized racism." Among Singleton's goals is to demonstrate "how Whiteness challenges the performance of students of color while shaping and reinforcing the racial perspective of White children." In workshops, principals and district superintendents were required to assess in writing their own degree of "white privilege."

Carranza's rhetoric about segregation and his push to change the admission criteria for the elite high schools (the state legislature did not give its needed approval) have stirred angry protests. His demotion of several high-ranking white female DOE officials and their replacement by African-American or Latino administrators sparked a May 2019 lawsuit against Carranza and the DOE, alleging violation of civil rights laws. A group of Asian-American parents demanded Carranza's dismissal—a demand echoed by the *New York Post*—asserting that proposed changes at the elite schools discriminate against Asian-American students who today constitute 74 percent of enrollment at Stuyvesant, 66 percent at Bronx Science. Those numbers could be cut in half under the chancellor's plan.

Unlike NYCHA, with its history of lying about problems, and the NYPD, with its emphasis on transparency and on reduction in crime, the DOE today remains an enigma to me. Speeches by de Blasio and Carranza often include words like segregation, inequality and privilege—overshadowing, even displacing time-honored educational goals like excellence, merit and improvement. When in fall 2018, Patrick Henry was honored as a best urban school (and gold winner) by the National Center for Urban School Transformation, the DOE did not bother to issue a press release.

My visits to and talks with schools and educators have only strengthened my original instinct: better outcomes for children in East Harlem will be determined school by school and classroom by classroom. For that to happen, top management must organize the system to zero in on how children learn, why they may not be learning—and then loosen the stifling strictures of bureaucracy, giving principals free rein to assemble the staffs they need to help children flourish.

In District 4. the examples of PS/IS 171, Dream, Success Academy Harlem 3, PS 83 and Central Park East High School show that with the right principal, dedication and no-excuse insistence on results, East Harlem schools can do a much better job. And yet, if my visits have shown me anything, it's that no single pedagogical method characterizes successful schools. From Dimitres Pantelidis' insistence on data to Dream's embrace of social-emotional learning to Success Academy's rigid classroom management (and unparalleled expectations of parental commitment) to Bennett Lieberman's rigorous attention to college prep, what these schools have in common are intangibles, hard to measure but nonetheless observable: genuine leadership, teamwork, teacher commitment, a deeply held conviction that all children entrusted to them must and will succeed.

Could the right schools and principals have prevented the personal tragedies that unfolded before us in the trial of Abraham Cucuta? Perhaps not every tragedy, but saving a life or two and rescuing a couple of young men from decades in prison would have been no small achievement.

CHAPTER 12

THE NONPROFIT ROLE IN EAST HARLEM

As a board member and volunteer at nonprofits involved in education and youth development, I've seen first-hand the impact that an excellent program can have on the lives of children. It's the rare head of a city agency who can match the passion of a nonprofit founder-entrepreneur, and few government programs, encumbered by layers of bureaucracy, display the creativity and dedication that the best nonprofits summon every day.

And yet when the problems of some young people begin before birth (inadequate prenatal care, mothers addicted to crack) and continue into their late teens, even the many dozens of nonprofits in East Harlem can only do so much.

After talking to or visiting nine of these organizations, I come away with the realization that whether their focus is early childhood, mental health therapy, after-school tutoring or rehabilitation of young men released from jail, the challenges are overwhelming in scale. As David

Garza, president of the venerable Henry Street Settlement (based on the Lower East Side, not in East Harlem) tells me, this kind of work "often feels like we're trying to empty the ocean of poverty one thimble at a time—while somebody smacks you in the elbow and somebody else yells at you that you're not doing it right."

One impressive, smaller nonprofit is LSA Family Health Service at 333 East 115th Street near First Avenue. LSA was founded in 1958 by the Little Sisters of the Assumption. With a budget of about $5 million, LSA today runs a food pantry; it also provides intensive services to 110 families with children from newborns to age three: home visits, nursing care, emotional support and interaction with other parents and young children.

When Asari Beale, director of communications, takes me on a tour and I see a group of mothers and toddlers in a playroom full of books and toys, it's easy to understand what a haven this can be for recent immigrants who have only a tenuous grasp of English, are socially isolated and have little ability to talk to, let alone ask for help from, city social service agencies. By bringing healthcare and emotional support directly to the homes of these mothers, LSA provides a level of care that they might otherwise never get.

In addition, for 25 children in grades K-3, LSA provides after-school tutoring and homework help, as well as a summer enrichment program, all with the help of volunteers from New York Cares.

Another nonprofit that punches well above its weight is Concrete Safaris, at East 115th Street and Lexington Avenue. Sharon (Mac) Levine, its hyper-energetic executive director, says she founded the organization in 2008 for a simple reason: East Harlem, along with the South

Bronx, "had the highest rates of childhood obesity and related diseases" in the city. Though Concrete Safaris had a budget of just $747,000, it serves hundreds of East Harlem children in a blend of after-school and summer activities. Among these are outdoor exercise, gardening in two NYCHA projects (in Jefferson Houses, Concrete Safaris reclaimed a lot that had been a dumping ground for discarded condoms and garbage), health promotion and community events.

Concrete Safaris also attracts 3,500 East Harlem residents to its Jungle Gym programs, five summer obstacle races and street fairs that it puts on in July and August. Through a three-year, $360,000 contract with the city's Department of Youth & Community Development, CS trains 250 to 260 young interns in its Outdoor Leadership Academy to staff summer health and exercise programs, and to run these community events. Of the total, 200 are ages 14 and 15; the balance are older. DYCD's Summer Youth Employment Program pays the wages of the older interns.

Levine explains that the interns are responsible for the events program: "They set it up, pack the trucks, lay out the race course in the streets, fill out the forms, and get the [people in the] community to pre-register. They literally do every single element of it." Even though some of the interns have never held a paying job before, Levine declares, "Hey, if they're 18 they should be able to learn how to do it." This is leadership training by doing.

Though Concrete Safaris has to hire up to eight temporary employees to oversee the school-year and summer programs—it has attracted funding from Deloitte, Merck Family Fund and Pinkerton Foundation, among others—its basic full-time staff consists of just four people. When

I ask how this is possible, Levine has a tongue-in-cheek, if cocky, answer: "We're pretty awesome."

At the other end of the nonprofit spectrum in size is Union Settlement Association, one of the city's oldest social service organizations. In East Harlem it covers the gamut from early childhood education (seven centers with a capacity of 444 children) to after-school tutoring (more than 300 children), college prep, job readiness and rehab counseling.

In 2018, 160 young men aged 16 to 24, some of whom have served time in jail, completed its two-week Career Academy job readiness program, with 100 percent gaining paid employment. David Nocenti, Union Settlement's executive director, speaks from experience when he explains, "If participants were told it was four times as long they would just walk away . . . we take people where they are." Of Union Settlement's $32.5 million budget, more than half comes from government grants, and Nocenti's previous stints as counsel to three New York State governors are undoubtedly an asset in navigating the political waters.

Two other large-scale providers of after-school and summer programs are Dream (formerly Harlem RBI) and East Harlem Tutorial Program (EHTP). In the past, Dream's after-school and summer programs, involving athletics, team-building and academics, have enrolled 1,200 young people in East Harlem, another 300 in the South Bronx and Newark.

EHTP has 700 children enrolled in its elementary, middle and high school programs; in recent years 100 percent of participating high school seniors have gone on to college, and, it claims, 84 percent of those in four-year colleges are on track to graduate within six years.

To Efrain Guerrero, chief of staff, and Alison Blazey, manager, data and research, an important element of success is if a student "is able to connect" and build a strong relationship with a staff member—an echo of Dimitres Pantelidis' comment, "It only takes one human being to change a child's life." Like Dream, EHTP also operates two charter schools in East Harlem.

Half a dozen nonprofits based in East Harlem deal with young people at risk of violence, or those released from jail and needing help putting their lives back together; typically these nonprofits take young men from all over the city. Besides Union Settlement, other East Harlem-based organizations working with ex-offenders include Exodus Transitional Community; Getting Out and Staying Out (GOSO) and its Cure Violence program, SAVE; and Supportive Children's Advocacy Network, or SCAN.

SCAN's executive director, Lew Zuchman, lays out for me his rationale for hiring ex-offenders: If you ask a young man coming out of jail what he wants, Zuchman says, the answer is almost always, "a job." So SCAN does its best to oblige. Zuchman puts me in touch with one such young man—let's call him Wilson—an amazing basketball player whom Zuchman hired to coach the neighborhood basketball team. As Wilson tells me about hanging out with the players before and after practice, it's evident he's imparting life lessons that could steer some of these young men away from the wrong activities.

The Pinkerton Foundation, a strong believer in such programs, has funded Exodus, GOSO, Friends of the Island and Bard Prison Initiative, among others. (Exodus, SAVE and GOSO are described in more detail in the section to follow, on criminal justice reform.)

"It's all about relationships" between counselors and the young men released from jail that makes for success, Laurie Dien, Pinkerton vice president and executive director for programs, explains. Pinkerton likes to help organizations that employ "credible messengers," people who were once incarcerated themselves and are now dedicated to mentoring others.

In the aggregate, the early childhood, after-school and summer recreation and team-building programs reach large numbers of young people in East Harlem. In the past, just two organizations, Dream and East Harlem Tutorial Program, have worked with well over 1,000 young people a year, nearly 10 percent of those enrolled in District 4 DOE schools. Measuring the impact of such programs, however, is notoriously difficult. Organizations can point to anecdotal success stories, and some statistical indicators of achievement, but I know of no attempt to document their collective impact on youth opportunity.

A big problem in these programs is the persistence rate and its inverse, the dropout rate. EHTP says its persistence rate for elementary and middle school students averages around 65 percent from year to year. At that rate, for every 100 children who join the program in first grade, only 12 will still be participating by grade 6.

The other, more serious problem, is whether supplementary programs can really help those children consigned to failing elementary and middle schools. One nonprofit leader willing to answer this question—and his answer is a resounding "no"—is Rich Berlin.

Berlin is the long-serving executive director of Harlem RBI. which several years ago renamed itself Dream. He grew up in the affluent northwest section of Washington, DC, moved to New York after college and began volunteering as a baseball coach at HRBI at age 25. That was in 1994, three years after HRBI had turned an abandoned, garbage-strewn lot in East Harlem into a ballfield and begun a baseball program for neighborhood kids.

In 1997 he became executive director, and by 1999, Harlem RBI was on its way to offering a full-fledged program of athletics, social and emotional development and team-building, including both summer and after-school tutoring and baseball.

Quite a few children in a given cohort—sometimes as many as 70 percent, Berlin estimates—stuck with the program all the way through middle school, graduated high school and went on to college. But when Berlin looked at the data, he found that the percentage of those graduating college within six years of admission was shockingly low—"in the teens."

The reasons? Money and geography, for one. Or, being the first generation of college-goers in their families. "But really the biggest factor," Berlin insists, "was that they all went to failing public schools their entire life."

It's this assessment that has led Dream to put nearly all its chips on Dream Charter School, Dream Charter High School and now, two new elementary-middle charter schools in the South Bronx. After 2019–20, the after-school program will be limited to just three legacy schools, though the summer baseball programs will continue.

"The future of our organization," Berlin says, "is extended-day, extended-year, multi-year schooling" that involves "rigorous academic and social-emotional learning." Being able to pass a standardized test is only one of several goals, he says, because what goes into being a full human being includes "all the things that go on outside of school with your family and your community that impact your character." The true comparison for Dream Charter School should not be other inner-city public schools, he continues, "but what our great schools in affluent communities look like."

Obviously not every nonprofit leader in East Harlem shares Berlin's diagnosis. Perhaps the performance of many children in District 4 schools would be even worse in the absence of supplementary programs. Perhaps tighter coordination with in-school instruction (a tough thing to pull off, given the DOE bureaucracy and the need to involve teachers) would lead to better results. But the reality is that while nonprofits in East Harlem are doing valiant work, they can't help everyone. Nor can they always they help enough, when enough is measured in time spent in an after-school program. For children far behind in school or in fractured families, three, four, even five hours a week may be too little and too late.

CHAPTER 13

CRIMINAL JUSTICE REFORM

What does it take to steer a teenager in East Harlem away from gang membership, away from shoplifting or robbery, away from violent acts? What does it take, once he's served time in jail, to give him a chance, a real chance, to get a job, to finish his education, and thus to avoid future arrests and incarceration? The answer to these questions will help determine the success or failure of criminal justice reform.

On the surface, such reform is underway in New York and elsewhere. Judges have accepted motions from the DAs in Manhattan, Queens, Brooklyn and the Bronx to dismiss 644,000 outstanding warrants, all at least ten years old, for minor charges ranging from marijuana possession to riding a bike on the sidewalk. And in January 2020, a new state law eliminated pretrial detention and bail for most misdemeanors and nonviolent felonies; the law will remove bail for 90 percent of those arrested. Meanwhile, the city jail population has declined steadily, from just under 11,700 in 2013 to a little under 6,000 at the end of December 2019, according to data from the Mayor's Office of Criminal Justice

More and more of those arrested, especially youthful offenders, are being offered supervised release, e.g., enrollment in a drug treatment or job readiness program, in lieu of incarceration.

There is significant funding for criminal justice reform. The Manhattan DA's office, which had raked in at least $808 million from huge settlements with banks accused of violating U.S. sanctions, is one source. The office funded five "youth opportunity hubs," one in East Harlem coordinated by Union Settlement, to the tune of $46 million and awarded an additional $12 million to nine community organizations that work with families and young people. Millions more are slated to go to organizations that can enhance and expand reentry services for released offenders. Another source of funds is the Mayor's Office of Criminal Justice, whose annual budget exceeds $125 million.

Eliminating bail for most offenses, releasing nonviolent prisoners early and championing supervised release instead of detention all have a nice ring to them. But the sticking point with such reforms is this: When young men are sent to alternative programs instead of to detention centers, they remain in their communities, tempted to hang out with the same crews, subject to the same peer pressure to engage in criminal behavior. Many have quit school early; too few have held a real job. If they return to the streets and get rearrested in large numbers, especially if they commit violent crimes, public support for criminal justice reform can ebb or even vanish.

(In the first two months of 2020, increases of 20 percent in the number of robberies, 8 percent in felony assaults and 20 percent in shooting incidents prompted the police commissioner and some district attorneys to call for changes in the new law. The proposed revisions would give judges more leeway to impose bail, especially for those accused of repeat or violent offenses.)

I think back to the testimony I heard in The People vs. Abraham Cucuta. Gabriel Washington and Alejandro Alvarez were each arrested multiple times; each lied multiple times to the cops; each ran away from one or more youth detention or drug treatment programs. In effect, each of them underwent various forms of supervised release, but the supervision was haphazard and ineffective, and the follow-up nonexistent. The crimes they committed affected innocent victims and all but ruined their own lives. Alvarez said he would have to leave the city to protect himself against gang retribution; Washington will be inside a prison cell until his mid-50s.

Connecting with young men before they commit a crime, or after they've been arrested and given an alternative to jail—this is the key need, the missing element in criminal justice reform. Which is where Omar Jackson and SAVE (Stand Against Violence East Harlem) come in.

It was after hearing Jackson's colleague, Javon Alexander, the outreach worker supervisor, describe SAVE at a 23rd Precinct Community Council meeting that I went to SAVE's offices to talk with Jackson and Alexander. The work of SAVE is easy to describe but success is hard to achieve. Jackson and his team talk to, share meals with and offer educational or job opportunities to these young men. At times their job requires moving quickly to dissuade someone from using a gun to retaliate for a shooting, or a supposed act of disrespect. The goal, instead, is to settle things with words, not bullets. In Jackson's words, he and his team try to find a way "to quash the beef."

He has no illusions that it is easy for a young man to change how he views himself, and to accept that there are alternatives to criminal behavior. In subsequent phone interviews, he tells me how difficult it is to reach the young men that SAVE is trying to help.

"You can't tell these guys nothing," Jackson says, "so it really has to come from within." The work is all about establishing rapport: "First of all they have to trust us 100 percent, because if I won't trust [you], I'm not sharing anything with you." And for every young man who does listen and who is open to an internship or a high school equivalency class, there are others who come by only for a free meal and a free Metrocard, not for help in changing their lives.

Still, change is possible, and the best example is Jackson himself. He is scrupulously honest about his own background, and what it took to transform himself from a young man committing crimes to an older, wiser man who tries to talk others out of doing so.

He grew up in Johnson Houses, raised by his mother and grandmother, having no contact with or even knowledge of his father. As a young teen he got involved in robbing people and stealing cars; later he headed a crew that sold crack cocaine and other drugs. Though not in a gang himself, he had close friends and associates, including those in his crew, who were members.

As he talks now about the life he once led, Jackson is frank about its appeal to an 18- or 19-year-old. He was his own boss and there was money, lots of it, money for cars and women. No supervisor told him what to do, no job required him to be at work at 9 A.M. and stay for eight hours.

"To tell the truth I was infatuated by the lifestyle," he says. He went to bed when he wanted, got up when he wanted, went out of town when he wanted. And only now does he recognize that he had an addiction, not to alcohol or drugs but to a way of life that was bound to lead to jail.

During these years, an older man, a sort of father figure, he says, gave him valuable advice: that even if he was determined to continue selling drugs, he should not be robbing people or harming them in any way, that it was wrong to hurt people. He took that advice to heart. What brought it home was being a robbery victim himself. Facing his assailants, one pointing a shotgun at him, the other a semi-automatic pistol, he realized his life could be over in a fraction of a second. Happily for him, the only cost of that incident was money.

The predictable result of selling drugs over a period of years was multiple arrests and incarceration. Jackson served two jail sentences totaling nearly five years. Even after the second release he had still not entirely abandoned crime.

But his attitudes and values were changing. Missing his son's first birthday because he was in jail had a big effect on him; years later he still talks of it with emotion. His wife Tawana was pushing him to get an education and a real job. Several years after his second release, he entered the Harlem division of College of New Rochelle, studied psychology and found he enjoyed reading, learning, wrestling with new ideas. He stuck with it and earned his Bachelor's. He joined SAVE in early 2016 and soon became committed to his new mission.

Now he says, "For me, working with my community, uplifting my community, helping my community—I am definitely passionate about this."

When I ask for a success story, he tells me about a young man, let's call him Gideon, released from Rikers at age 19 who talked to a SAVE outreach worker.

"He was really lost, trying to find himself, and amongst us he would let us know, 'I don't want to be involved'" in crime. When he was with his friends, however, "he felt he couldn't tell them."

SAVE helped find Gideon a job in construction, got him medical attention for mental health problems. He also passed his high school equivalency exam and is in the process of moving into his own apartment.

Gideon "has gotten his act together and we are all extremely proud of him," Jackson says. Then he adds, "And we hope he keeps it up because that's a challenge."

Another crucial aspect of making criminal justice reform work is helping young men released from Rikers and upstate prisons to lead productive lives and stay out of jail. This too has to be done one-on-one, and Getting Out and Staying Out (GOSO), SAVE's parent organization, has a proven formula for success, based on what it calls the 3E's: education, employment, emotional support.

GOSO starts working with prisoners when they are in Rikers. After release, each participant gets his own career manager—there are eight of them, all licensed social workers—and then begins a two-week job readiness program. Mark Goldsmith, founder of GOSO, would insist that after completing that program, each man had to show up for a personal interview, dressed in suit and tie and prepared to talk about his future. Those who pass are automatically eligible for a paid internship, with

GOSO picking up the tab. (Goldsmith stepped down as chief executive in 2020 but will stay involved with the organization. The new CEO, Jocelynne Rainey, was chief administrative officer at the Brooklyn Navy Yard Development Corporation, and architect of its workforce development program.)

The internships often lead to full-time employment, and GOSO carefully cultivates relationships with employers willing to take on its participants. One enthusiastic partner is Dos Toros, the fast-growing chain of California-style Mexican tacquerias, which has employed dozens of GOSO participants, including a 31-year-old who now manages one of its midtown restaurants.

Besides the internships and the individual counseling, GOSO also has classrooms, staffed by DOE teachers, where the young men can study for their high school equivalency diploma; a number have gone on to college.

When I get the opportunity to listen to ten current and former participants sit around a table and talk about their experiences, I'm struck by how many of them refer to GOSO as a family and its offices as a second home; the organization has managed to create an atmosphere of compassion and caring that is palpable to a visitor.

And, though the rate of recidivism is notoriously hard to calculate, GOSO says the percentage of its participants who return to jail is only 15 percent, far below rates that can range from the mid-40s to as high as 75 percent in various jurisdictions around the U.S.

Half a dozen or more nonprofits in New York also offer re-entry services to released inmates. Two of the largest are Fortune Society and Osborne Association, each with a budget approaching $40 million per year.

One nonprofit that has a similar feel and approach to GOSO is Exodus Transitional Community on Third Avenue near East 123rd Street, only blocks from GOSO.

Begun by Julio Medina, who earned a Bachelor's from SUNY-Albany during his 12 years in prison, Exodus deals with an even more challenging population: men (and some women) who have typically served much longer prison sentences than those released from Rikers. The same sense of community, of clients feeling at home and cared for, pervades its offices. Ninety percent of Exodus staff are themselves ex-offenders, and they know the first questions to ask a newcomer: "Where did you sleep last night? Have you eaten today?"

I sit in on a session in Exodus' Re-Entry Wilderness Program, two weeks of "soft skills" and job readiness training. Here I watch facilitator Phillip White engage eight men, older than the GOSO participants, as they rehearse for a job interview. With a combination of humor, detailed coaching and exacting standards, White has each man go around the room addressing each of his fellow participants as if introducing himself to a prospective employer. Maintaining the right physical distance from the employer, smiling, shaking hands firmly, describing concisely and respectfully what he can do to fill the job—this is the approach that White wants, and he insists that the participants do it over and over until they get it right.

Both GOSO and Exodus have annual budgets of between $4.5 million and $5 million, half from government contracts, the balance from foundations and private donors. Based on 500 active participants, Geoff Golia, GOSO's associate executive director, figures its cost per participant at $7,500 in the first year, which includes the salaries of a paid internship. In subsequent years the cost drops to $3,500. Compared to the price tag of detaining someone in a New York City jail, it seems money well spent. The city Department of Corrections budget in fiscal 2019 was $1.4 billion. Based on an average jail population of 7,000, that's *$200,000* per inmate, or 60 times GOSO's cost. (A report from the City Comptroller's office puts the cost for the Rikers Island jails even higher, at $337,500 per inmate per year.)

My visits to SAVE, GOSO and Exodus leave me with a sense of hope about what can be accomplished, but an even stronger awareness of the magnitude of the problem.

It's hard, wrenching work for a young man of 18 or 20 to abandon the habits and behavior learned on the streets or with gang buddies and embrace the need for change. It's even harder for a man of 40, released after 15 years for armed robbery or manslaughter.

One of the GOSO clients, a young man named Tim, talks to me about how he showed up at GOSO in 2012 or 2013 to hear about the program and then left without coming back. Four years later, dealing with several unresolved arrest warrants, he finally returned to GOSO to acknowledge that yes, he needed help. GOSO arranged for a lawyer to represent him at his first court appearance. He completed the two-week job readiness program, got one-on-one counseling, and now has a full-time job at a restaurant in Brooklyn, while also working odd jobs to supplement his restaurant salary and to afford an apartment. His experience illustrates how some men have to exhaust all other possibilities before they realize that help is available but that they must reach out and ask for it.

CHAPTER 14

AFTERWORD: JURORS, LAWYERS, THE JUDGE

For the jurors, even a trial that lasts several weeks is a brief interlude in a life. A year after the trial ended, I check in with my fellow jurors and find that, at least for a few of them, the experience of The People vs. Abraham Cucuta retains an emotional impact that survives the months that have elapsed.

Sofia, now 27, the tall blond woman who stood at the blackboard in the jury room recording the guilty/not guilty votes, is still at PS 89 in Elmhurst, Queens; this elementary school has nearly 2,000 students, 73 percent of them Hispanic. She works with fifth graders whose native language is not English.

About the trial, she says, "I'm glad that I did it and I'm sorry that it had to end that way, but he [the defendant] made a choice."

Recalling the eyewitnesses at trial who cut school for months at a time, I ask what, if anything, a teacher can do to help locate these students and get them back in school.

"If one kid just disappears for weeks," she says, "that really is a big red flag."

Nevertheless, teachers have their hands full, she points out. Is it reasonable to ask them to also serve as social workers and family counselors?

"I love my students," she adds, in a remark that is both wistful and honest, "but at the end of the day they're not my responsibility."

Marc, now 46, has landed a new job as portfolio manager at Millennium Management, a major hedge fund that has $34 billion under management. Though a self-described skeptic about the criminal justice system (originally he told me, "If you have enough money you can literally get away with murder"), now he says, "I wish more people would try to serve, as opposed to getting out of jury duty. I think people would find the process enlightening."

His final thought about the trial: "I think we convicted the person responsible for a double murder but I do not think justice was served . . . We as a society have failed those born into difficult circumstances."

Harvey, retired from the clothing business, is preoccupied with family. He spent several years caring for his 93-year old mother, who passed away in December 2019, and he and his wife stay in close touch with their only child, a daughter in her sophomore year at Goucher.

Has he thought much about the trial and its meaning?

"Actually, I have," says Harvey.

He continues to dwell on the fact that "two young men were brutally assassinated" by a murderer who, he believes, deserves no sympathy or compassion. And he wonders how we as a society can allow generation after generation to grow up in the kind of family circumstances and violent neighborhoods described in the trial—with the result that some young people "put no value at all" on human life.

Emily, the real estate broker at Compass, is dealing with a down-market in real estate by maintaining her upbeat approach to life and work: "Things turn around and come back stronger, that's the history." Despite the slowdown in sales, a client of hers closed on deal to buy a $9.5 million condo in a new development on West 81st Street. A smaller deal, for a condo in Tribeca, is in the works.

Reflecting on her jury experience now, she says "It's had its impact. I live in a very different world than those who were involved" in the 2007 murders. "It's important never to take that for granted."

Kristen is another juror who thinks about how different her life is from that of the participants in the trial. In the intervening months she finished her MBA and left a big healthcare communications consulting firm to go with a small startup.

"I don't have any regrets about the verdict, though I do think about the trial often," she says. "It is still upsetting to know that that our neighborhoods are so dramatically divided, and shocking that socio-economic class defines what people are exposed to."

The professionals from the trial, both prosecutor and defense attorney are back to what they do; only the names and circumstances change. Dafna Yoran was tapped to direct the prosecution of James Jackson, a white supremacist who traveled from Baltimore to New York in March 2017 for the express purpose of killing black men. But unlike the Cucuta case, this one ended with a quick arrest and no trial. On January 23, 2019 Jackson pleaded guilty to murder as terrorism and murder as a hate crime in the fatal stabbing of Timothy Caughman, 66 on March 20, 2017. Jackson had turned himself in to police shortly after the murder. He faces life in prison without parole.

No doubt the DA's office will find other challenging assignments for Yoran, although with the number of homicides in the city down by 41 percent since 2007, she may find herself with fewer murderers to hold accountable for their crimes. In fact, the number of homicide prosecutions brought to trial in Manhattan has declined along with the murder rate: from 25 in 2007 and 26 in 2008 to just 16 in 2018.

As for Dawn Florio, the tough cases keep coming. In Queens she is defending Barry Hall, accused with a co-defendant, Pharoah Ferguson of second degree murder and attempted second degree murder in the January 28, 2018 killing of Sherwood Beverly and the wounding of others who were sitting in a car with Beverly. And in the Bronx, she represents Joselin Espada, 38, accused of shooting to death a cousin, George Carrasquillo in the early hours of February 5, 2018. Both cases were the subject of numerous adjournments, with the next court appearances scheduled for sometime in 2020.

And Judge Michael Obus is back on the bench in courtroom 1324 at 100 Centre Street, as a New York State Supreme Court Justice, criminal branch. After reaching the normal retirement age of 70, he was appointed by Governor Cuomo to a special two-year term to fill a vacancy, and is eligible for two more such terms.

Among other cases, he presided over a high-profile trial arising from a deadly gas explosion in the East Village in March 2015 that killed two men, ages 23 and 26, and injured 13 other people. An illegal gas hookup, authorized by a greedy building owner and carried out by a plumber, led to the subsequent leak and the explosion. In November 2019, the jury found three defendants, including the owner and the plumber, guilty of manslaughter and criminally negligent homicide.

In sentencing each defendant to between four and twelve years in prison, Judge Obus said, "The defendants did, in a matter of speaking, roll the dice on the lives of these people,"

The judge had no reason in this moment to recall the Cucuta trial, whose origin was a dice game in the courtyard of East River Houses. But for me the coincidence of that dice game that ended two lives and changed others (mine included) and the metaphorical rolling of the dice that caused the East Village gas explosion and two premature deaths, is too pointed to ignore. In one sense, chance determines when human beings die, but in both these cases it was the criminal choices made by other people that cut short young lives

CHAPTER 15

A LETTER AND SOME ANSWERS

In November 2018, I wrote a letter to Abraham Cucuta offering to visit him in federal prison in Pennsylvania, not to rehash or even discuss his trial but to learn more about him and his family.

The idea behind the letter was simple yet simple-minded; I thought that if I could get Cucuta to talk about how he grew up, where he lived, what schools he attended, who his friends were and even, how he came to join the Bloods and begin selling crack cocaine, perhaps he would see the murder trial as the inevitable culmination of a series of life choices—choices that he either made voluntarily, or that were forced upon him. After all, in the sweep of human history it is a blink of an eye, half a dozen or a dozen generations, since the time when most young men learned a trade or farmed a piece of land because their fathers had done so. For those generations, the essence of men's and women's lives was not choice but destiny. Tragic as it sounds, it's possible that for Cucuta too, the outcome of the life he lived was destiny.

I was at his sentencing in February 2018 when Cucuta (Holiday to his friends and enemies), had ranted at the police, the prosecutors and the eyewitnesses who had identified him as the shooter, denying all responsibility for killing two men. I never imagined that if he talked to me he would acknowledge his guilt; instead I wanted to see him not just as a killer but as a person.

When I raised my hand in Judge Obus' courtroom on November 20, 2017 to indicate that I was willing to serve, the odds were against my being picked for the jury. First it took the roll of a drum for a card with my name on it to be plucked by the clerk and read aloud. Then it took a one-in-five chance for prosecutors and the defense counsel to accept me as an impartial juror.

Never mind what people say as they are questioned in open court; no one selected as a juror can be completely impartial. Like many people I believe that when the police arrest a suspect and the prosecutors charge him with a crime, there is usually *some* basis for the indictment and arrest. Yet I'm also aware that the basis may be wrong or the evidence too flimsy, too inconclusive to take away a person's liberty. I shouldered my responsibility seriously, which was to weigh the testimony and, to the best of my ability, to give the defendant the presumption of innocence. So did my fellow jurors.

But after hearing from the first eyewitness, Gabriel Washington, who crouched a foot or two away from two men gunned down in cold blood on June 7, 2007, my view of the trial began to change.

One reason for serving was my desire to write about the experience of being a juror in a murder trial. Listening to the story of Washington's life, and then, a few days later, the even more harrowing ordeal of Alejandro

Alvarez, made me realize that I would have to write about something more important than the innocence or guilt of Abraham Cucuta. I would have to write about why this crime took place. Why Washington and Alvarez and Cucuta lived the lives and made the choices they did. Why East River Houses—seedy, decrepit, neglected—was an incubator of drug-selling and violence. Why shootings occur and neighbors or witnesses are afraid to tell the cops who did them. Why so many children from this NYCHA project enter PS 146 and other schools in East Harlem and eight years later lack the basic literacy in math and English that could prepare them for success in a modern economy.

And how and why single mothers like Denikqua Berry, Lisa Torres and hundreds of others, do their best to shield their sons and daughters from the dangers of the streets and to enroll them in a handful of schools where these children can succeed.

I had all this in mind when I sent my letter to Abraham Cucuta. I didn't expect an answer and I got none.

One of Abraham's brothers, Edgardo Cucuta, also has an arrest record but as of this writing was not in jail. Using his last known address, given to me by police sources, I make a final visit to East River Houses, this time to a ground-floor apartment in Building 401. The woman who answers my knock tells me there is no Edgardo Cucuta living there, that she does not know Edgardo Cucuta, nor does she know anyone who might. When she shuts the door I linger for ten minutes in the darkened lobby, asking passersby if the name Edgardo Cucuta means anything to them. It's hard to believe there's no one who can say yes.

Nevertheless, despite my inability to speak with Abraham Cucuta or his brother, I have gotten at least partial answers to my other questions. I've learned, in the most vivid of terms, how much parents (including single parents) or grandparents matter. Learned that a child like Gabriel Washington, orphaned at 12 and cutting school day after day with no consequences, can easily end up as a drug seller and then graduate to gang membership and adult crime. That a boy like Alejandro Alvarez, obese and bullied, with a mother who is a crack addict and a father who leaves him, a six-year-old, alone for days in charge of younger siblings, may choose to flee home and school to wind up on the streets, sleeping in subways and robbing tourists. With such a background, is it a surprise that eventually he became the right-hand man to a drug crew boss who gunned down two victims in a moment of unprovoked rage?

I've learned that the combination of badly deteriorated public housing projects, families that are often headed by single mothers, children in foster care because there is no parent or an unfit or incarcerated parent, and a culture of poverty that is transmitted from generation to generation, makes for fertile ground for gangs, violence and ruined lives.

I've learned that the cops, for all the suspicion and criticism (sometimes justified) they engender, have reduced and continue to reduce crime in neighborhoods like East Harlem, and that they are reaching out to residents in ways that may make these neighborhoods safer still.

And I've learned that educators like Dimitres Pantelidis, Eve Colavito, Tara Stant and Bennett Lieberman are succeeding with the very young people whom other principals and teachers are failing to reach. I don't blame the other teachers and principals. I blame the Chancellor of the New York City Department of Education, the Mayor and political leaders who hide behind slogans (including blaming principals and district superintendents for the supposed sin of "white privilege"), offer excuses and shy away from the hard work, the work of years: first, to identify and recruit leaders who can make a difference, school by school, classroom by classroom; then to provide them the freedom and resources to do so.

To me it doesn't matter whether the schools that work for children are regular DOE schools or charter schools or Catholic schools or private schools with a unique mission. What matters is that schools that succeed are supported, and schools that fail are not tolerated.

Unfortunately, instead of appreciating the crucial role of principals, mayors usually focus their attention on hiring the school chancellor, often some heralded miracle worker from out of town who is supposed to transform the school system from above. In fact, since 1993, a period of 26 years, there have been eight school chancellors with an average tenure of just over three years. And yet it can take the right principal five years or more to turn around a failing school.

So instead of the inevitable hunt in 2021 or 2022 for the next chancellor, consider what would happen if the city conducted an *annual*, nationwide search for 25 exceptional principals to serve in the city's neediest schools. Some of them could be found right here in New York. They would each be hired for five years and given free rein to assemble the teaching staff they need. After four years of such an effort, imagine the impact that 100 exceptional principals could have, some of them in East and Central Harlem, some in other poor areas like the South Bronx, or Brownsville and East New York in Brooklyn.

The finale of my story as juror number 2 in The People vs. Abraham Cucuta is simply this: The jury system works at assessing innocence or guilt, but public institutions too often fail at the daunting job of social repair and uplift. They fail not for lack of good intentions but because over and over they do the same things and offer the same solutions that haven't worked in the past.

Whether the issue is how to remedy the disastrous state of the NYCHA projects, how to improve the quality of education offered to every child in New York, with special attention to those in the greatest need, how to make unsafe neighborhoods safer or how to stem the inexorable rise in homelessness (a major cause of family distress and of children's difficulties in school), those in power are seemingly never at a loss for answers. They're quick to propose new programs with grandiose names and very large price tags, as if the mere enunciation of such efforts is a guarantee of success. Far better to approach these challenges with humility, a willingness to start small, a recognition that the quick answer and the big budget are often the wrong answer and the waste of valuable resources.

Lasting social change often begins at the grass roots. It requires true community leaders to emerge; they may be educators, social workers, business people, mental health professionals or local residents; not only do they know the problems but they are already working on the solutions. Change in a neighborhood like East Harlem, like so many other poor areas of the city, demands both urgency and patience, the urgency to begin today, the patience to engage in trial and error, recognizing that there is no quick fix for social pathologies that have been decades in the making.

And yet, the signposts of progress are there, if only we can draw the right lessons from them.

Not far from the East River Houses courtyard where two men were shot to death playing dice, crime rates are falling, schools like PS 171, Success Academy Harlem 3 and Central Park East High School are succeeding against long odds, and organizations like Getting Out and Staying Out and Exodus Transitional Community are doing their best to meet the heroic challenge of preparing young men (as well as older ex-offenders) released from jail to live productive lives. The successes are real but sparse; the question is how to multiply their numbers five-fold, then ten-fold. The real crime would be to waste the lives of too many more children in East Harlem before we act on the lessons of those successes.

INDEX

Agard, Joshua (Josh), 16–18, 25, 28, 30, 34, 37, 38, 39, 50, 51, 53, 63, 65, 67, 72
Alexander, Javon, 13, 121
Alvarez, Alejandro, 15–16, 25, 29, 37, 40–53, 54, 63, 64, 84–86, 121, 134–136
America's Best Urban Schools award, 102, 109
Asian-American parents, 108

Banner, 51
Beale, Asari, 112
Berish, Joshua, Detective, 84–85
Berlin, Rich, 116–118
Berry, Denikqua, 99, 135
Betzy (Cucuta girlfriend), 46
Bharara, Preet, U.S. Attorney, 78
Blazey, Alison, 115
Bloods (gang), 15–17, 25, 34, 38, 47, 49
Bloomberg, Michael, 105–106
Booga, see Rudolph, Wyatt
Bratton, Bill, NYPD Commissioner, 78, 83
Brown, Alexandra, 96–97

Carranza, Richard, 107–108
Castillo, Frances, 93
Catholic schools, 100
Cellphones, cellphone towers, 29, 59, 64, 65
Central Park East High School, 94–95, 99, 109, 139
Chancellor (DOE), 105–109, 137

Charlett (mother of Wyatt Rudolph), 49
Charter schools, 94–99
Christen (juror), 23
Cohn, Rachel, 90
Colavito, Eve, 95–96, 136
CompStat, 83–84
Concrete Safaris, 112–114
Cooperation agreement, 19, 35, 48
Covenant House, 43
Criminal justice reform, 119–127
Crime, East Harlem and NYC, 78–80. See also, NYPD
Crips (gang), 15–17, 25, 49
Cruz, Jose, 69
Cruz, Vanessa, 69–72
Cucuta, Abraham, 18, 25, 27–29, 37–39, 41, 46–47, 49–53, 58, 61–65, 70–72, 74, 79, 85, 86, 121, 132–135
Cucuta, Edgardo, 135

De Blasio, Bill, 107
Dice game, 15
District Attorney's office (Manattan), 36
District 4, see DOE
Deuteronomy, Book of, 40
Dien, Laurie, 115–116
DOE, 73, 86–110, 118, 136
Double A, see Alvarez, Alejandro
Dream, Dream Charter School, 95–97, 109, 114, 116–118
Dunn, Billy, Detective, 52, 79

East Harlem, 22, 84, 87, 89, 137–138
 East Harlem crime, see NYPD
 East Harlem NYCHA projects, see NYCHA
 East Harlem schools, see DOE
East Harlem Tutorial Program, 114–116
East River Houses, 15–17, 21, 28–29, 31–32, 34, 36–37, 41, 43, 45–46, 49, 51 74–80, 83, 139
East Village gas explosion, trial, 131–132
Emily (juror), 22, 130
Estrella, Alexandra, 99
Exodus Transitional Community, 115, 126, 139

Fariña, Carmen, 107
Figaro, Joanne, 75–76
Florio, Dawn, attorney, 19, 26–28, 41, 47, 53, 54–56, 60, 67, 131
Fortune Society, 125

Gangs, gang code, gang membership, gang retribution, 14–15, 19, 21, 25, 29, 32, 34, 36, 39, 47, 49, 52, 54, 72–73, 78, 85–87, 119, 121–122, 127, 136
Garza, David, 111–112
Geager, Hector, 104
Getting Out and Staying Out, see GOSO
Goldsmith, Mark, 13, 124–125
Golia, Geoff, 126
"Good enough," mentality of, 101–102
Gonzalez, George, 91
GOSO, 13–14, 115, 124–127, 139
Graham, Dr. Jason, medical examiner, 29
Guerrero, Efrain, 115

Harlem RBI, see Dream
Harvey (juror), 23, 129–130
Henry Street Settlement, 112
Holiday, see Cucuta
How Children Succeed, 103
How the Other Half Learns, 98

Jackson, Omar, 13, 14, 121–124
Jefferson Houses, 13, 14, 78, 83
JHS117, 43

John (alternate juror), 23
Johnson Houses, 13, 14, 122
Johnson, Joseph, 102
Joselina (juror), 23, 63–65
Jurors, jury duty, 18, 21, 22, 24, 138. *See also* individual jurors

Kearse, Michael, 25, 34–36, 49, 52
KIPP charter network, 103
Klein, Joel, 105
Kowal, Susan, 93–94
Kristen (juror), 23, 64, 130

Leadership, urban school systems, 105
Levin, David, 103
Levine, Mac, 112–114
Lieberman, Bennett, 94–95, 109, 136
"Look Beyond Stuyvesant," 104
LSA Family Health Service, 112
Lujan, Angel, Detective, 81
Lynch, James, ADA, 25–26, 41, 49

Manhattan DA's Office, 120
Manhattan Village Academy, 104
Marc (juror), 23, 62, 129
Mayor's Office of Criminal Justice, 120
Medina, Julio, 126
Melissa (alternate juror), 23
Mellusi, Adam, Lieutenant, 81–82
Metropolitan Hospital, 44
Miguel (juror), 23
Moskowitz, Eva, 97

Nakia (alternate), 23
National Center for Urban School Transformation, 102, 109
New York City Dept. of Corrections, 127
New York City Dept. of Education, see DOE
New York City Dept. of Youth & Community Development, 113
New York City Housing Authority, see NYCHA
New York City Police Dept., see NYPD
New York State Supreme Court, 18
Nocenti, David, 114
Nonprofits, East Harlem, 111–118
NYCHA, 15, 73–78, 108, 138
NYPD, 73, 75, 78–79, 81–85, 108

Obus, Michael, Judge, 18, 23–24, 40, 60–61, 64–65, 72, 74, 131–132, 134
O'Keefe, David, ADA, 48, 52
Oliver Twist, 45
Olivia (juror), 23, 62, 67
100 Centre St., 18, 20, 21, 52, 131
O'Neill, James, NYPD Commissioner, 84
Osborne Association, 125

PCP (angel dust), 47
Panetta, Michael, 93
Pantelidis, Dimitres, 89–94, 102, 109, 136
People vs. Abraham Cucuta, 19, 56, 121, 128, 138
Phoenix House, 46
PIRU (Pimps in Red Uniforms), 16, 25, 49
Pinkerton Foundation, 115–116
Pitman, Dwight, 79
Pondiscio, Robert, 98
Precinct 23, *see* NYPD
PreK program, 101
Price, Richard, 77–79
Principals, importance of, search for, trust in, 99–104, 106, 109–110, 136–137, 139
PS 12 TAG Young Scholars, 88
PS 37 River East, 93
PS 83 Luis Munoz Rivera, 93, 99, 109
PS 146, 43, 99, 100
PS/IS 171 Patrick Henry, 88–93, 99, 102, 109, 139
PSA 5, *see* NYPD

Rainey, Jocelynne, 125
Ravitch, Diane, 106
Rikers Island (jail), 13, 14, 46, 127
Rodriguez, Robert, State Assemblyman, 100–101
Roldan, Neris, 90
Rudolph, Wyatt, 18, 26, 28, 37, 38, 50, 64

Sabater, Manuel (Manny), 16–18, 25–26, 28, 30, 32, 34, 36–38, 50–51, 53, 63–65, 67, 71–72, 74
Sam (juror), 23, 65
SAVE, 13–14, 121–124

SCAN (Supportive Children's Advocacy Network), 115
Shea, Dermot, NYPD Commissioner, 85
Shyce, *see* Kearse, Michael
Silfen, Mona, 99
SMM (Sex Money Murder), 16, 25, 34, 37, 49
Sophia (juror), 23, 63, 128
Specialized High Schools Admission Test (SHSAT), 104
Stand Against Violence-East Harlem, *see* SAVE
Stant, Tara, 97–98, 102, 136
Steiner, David, 106–107
Stuyvesant High School, 104, 108
Success Academy, Success Academy Harlem 3, 97–99, 102, 109, 139

Test scores, *see* DOE, *see* Charter schools
    Test scores, racial disparities, 88, 104
Thomas, Wilfred. 76
Torres, Lisa, 69, 99, 135
Torres, Maria, 69–71
Tough, Paul, 103
Tripp, 49

Union Settlement, 114
United Federation of Teachers, 106

Vance, Cyrus, Manhattan DA, 78
Vega, Michael, officer, 81

Washington, Gabriel (Gabes), 16, 25, 27, 29, 31–41, 50–51, 54, 63, 86, 121, 134–136
Washington Houses, 78–79, 83
Weingarten, Randi, 106
White, Phillip, 126
"White privilege" workshops, 108
Wilson Houses, 16–17, 25, 31, 78

Yakatally, Amir, Deputy Inspector, 85
Yoran, Dafna, ADA, 19, 25, 31–32, 37–38, 48, 56–59, 60, 65, 130–131
Yoran, Shalom, 57
Yoran, Varda, 59

Zuchman, Lew, 115

ABOUT THE AUTHOR

Efrem Sigel's first novel, ***The Kermanshah Transfer*** (Macmillan), came out in 1973. Thirty-five years later, ***The Disappearance*** was published by The Permanent Press. ***Juror Number 2: The Story of a Murder, the Agony of a Neighborhood*** (The Writers' Press) is his first book-length memoir. A third novel and a collection of previously published short stories are both in progress. More than 30 of his stories and memoirs have appeared in dozens of magazines, including *The Journal*, the *Antioch Review*, the *Jerusalem Post*, *Midstream*, *Nimrod*, *Sixfold*, *Gemini*, and *PerSe,* and have won a number of prizes.

Sigel has been a journalist, editor and founder of two business publishing companies. He lives in New York City. He's a project coordinator for the Harvard Business School Club of NY Community Partners program, in which HBS alumni, as volunteers, provide pro bono consulting to nonprofits in the field of education. He's a member of the board of directors of Futures and Options, a nonprofit that arranges intensive orientation, paid internships and career exploration for students from underserved neighborhoods in New York City.

EFREM SIGEL'S WORKS

Juror Number 2: The Story of a Murder, the Agony of a Neighborhood, The Writers' Press, 2020

Compulsively readable, a true crime story and an expose that takes you into the neighborhoods, housing projects, police precincts and schools in East Harlem to show the problems faced by young people growing up here-and to highlight what's working amidst so much that isn't.

The Disappearance, The Permanent Press, 2009

When Joshua and Nathalie Sandler's only child, 14-year-old Daniel, disappears one flawless summer day in a tiny hamlet in western Massachusetts, their world changes in an instant.

"Powerful and elegantly crafted. Subtle and probing."
—*Publishers Weekly* ★ starred review.

"Gripping, emotional and tender. Has a deep emotional core that will resonate with any reader."—*Booklist*

"A wonderful novel-profoundly imagined, beautifully written. A remarkable achievement."—*Max Byrd,* acclaimed historical novelist

The Kermanshah Transfer: A Novel of Middle Eastern Intrigue, Macmillan, 1973

In the last years of the Shah, on the cusp of the Islamic revolution, an American working in Tehran finds himself in the midst of a gun-smuggling plot involving Kurds, Israelis, Iranians and Iraqis

For more information and to order any of these books, go to: www.thewriterspress.com

Printed in Great Britain
by Amazon